WRESTLING

★★★ AT ★★★

THE CHASE

BY
ED WHEATLEY

REEDY PRESS

Chase Hotel and Park Plaza

THE CHASE PARK PLAZA

HOME IN THE HEART OF ST. LOUIS

WRESTLING
★ ★ ★ AT ★ ★ ★
THE CHASE

BY
ED WHEATLEY

REEDY PRESS

Library of Congress Control Number: 2021935132

ISBN: 9781681063447

Cover design: Eric Marquard

Interior design: Eric Marquard and Linda Eckels

All interior images are courtesy of Herb Simmons unless otherwise noted.

Front cover images courtesy (*clockwise*) Herb Simmons, Getty Images, Getty Images, Getty Images, Getty Images, Getty Images, (*center images*) Herb Simmons

Back cover images courtesy (*left to right, top row*) Herb Simmons, Herb Simmons, Herb Simmons, Getty Images, Herb Simmons, Getty Images, (*left to right, bottom row*) Getty Images, Herb Simmons, Getty Images, Wikimedia Commons, Vicki Martin, Bob Garagiola

Timeline images (*left to right, top row*) Media Museum, Brian Walsh, Herb Simmons, Media Museum, Herb Simmons, Wikimedia Commons, Herb Simmons, Bob Garagiola (*left to right, bottom row*) Herb Simmons, Missouri Historical Society, Herb Simmons, Brian Walsh, Wikimedia Commons, Wikipedia, Herb Simmons

Printed in the United States of America
21 22 23 24 25   5 4 3 2 1

DEDICATION

N 2005, LARRY MATYSIK, the longtime voice of *Wrestling at the Chase*, wrote a book titled *Wrestling at the Chase: The Inside Story of Sam Muchnick and the Legends of Professional Wrestling*. It was a collection of tales about his involvement with the popular Saturday night wrestling program. Larry dreamed of having a coffee table–style book that captured the history of the program and brought to life the men and women who made it a success. He wanted the book filled with hundreds of pictures and stories so that the generations who watched the show could reminisce with happy memories while new generations could experience and appreciate its legacy. Larry died in 2018 before that could happen. It is now my great pleasure to complete that dream and take readers back to one of the greatest sports and theatrical programs of all time.

This book is also dedicated to Ted Koplar. Ted had carried on what his father and grandfather began in the operations of the Chase Park Plaza and KPLR-TV. Ted provided many insights for the early drafts of this book but unfortunately passed away before its completion. It is hoped that Sam, Larry, and Ted shall forever be remembered by the rekindled memories offered in these pages.

Dick the Bruiser wrestles Bobby Duncan to the floor in a tag team match while Duncan's partner, Blackjack Lanza helplessly watches from the ropes.
COURTESY OF GETTY IMAGES

CONTENTS

The Garibaldi
Brothers

INTRODUCTION

HOW AMAZING IS IT that the mere mention of four simple words, *Wrestling at the Chase*, can immediately bring back fond memories of the magical moments of a television program that left the airwaves nearly 40 years ago. Ask anyone over the age of 50 about the program and they will immediately respond with stories that go on for several minutes. For nearly three decades, generations of fans across the Midwest were drawn to their television sets each weekend. Whether they were lucky enough to be ringside with the hottest ticket in town or at home watching on television, the memories endure. Even though the last bell was rung decades ago, vivid memories of fans' favorite wrestlers and storylines have been passed along to their children and grandchildren so that the legacy of *Wrestling at the Chase* survives to this day.

The greatest epitaph of the program is one written by those stars still with us who climbed into the ring and created those many memories. As a lead-in to the *Wrestling at the Chase* story, four former wrestlers have provided their thoughts on what it meant to be a part of one of America's all-time top sporting events. Here in their words is what *Wrestling at the Chase* meant then and now:

"IT IS MY PLEASURE to lend a little of my experience. As you know, we all loved Sam (Muchnick) and St. Louis. Even though I only wrestled at the Chase after the televised matches were moved from the ballroom to the studio, it was still the best. St. Louis was the place you wanted to make it to. Wrestling in St. Louis had a long history of hosting the greatest wrestlers in the world, including such greats like Ed "Strangler" Lewis, Lou Thesz, John Pesek, Pat O'Connor, and many others. Beside the legends of the past, you could be sure the best of the present would be there. You've heard all those stories from all of us over the years. Thanks for what you have done to keep those memories alive."

—**Baron Von Raschke**

"ST. LOUIS WAS A GREAT wrestling town. I myself only met Sam a few times in my wrestling career, but my dad worked for him many times—in fact, he was on the first televised show in 1959. Everyone wanted to work St. Louis. It was said that if you made it to St. Louis with Sam, you made it to the big times. Not only did Sam require it, the workers gave their best to the fans. Then you had others that helped make the show a hit—Joe Garagiola, Mickey Garagiola, and of course the person I believe was the best play-by-play announcer ever, Larry Matysik. That and the best talent in the USA made *Wrestling at the Chase* the best."

—**"Cowboy" Bob Orton**

"WRESTLING AT THE CHASE was so special. It wasn't like a normal studio that we always worked—it had an historical sense. All the greats worked there. You always picked up your game when working at the Chase. You knew if you didn't there were always others just waiting to steal your spot. We all knew if you made it to St. Louis, you made it to the big time. Working there meant you had made it to the next level. St. Louis was the top venue, so being at the Chase was the best of the best."

—**Jerry Brisco**

"IN THE YEAR 1978, Terry Funk told me if I wanted to be a star in this business, I had to get to St. Louis on Friday night. You know what I'm talking about. I had to be at the Kiel or the Arena, I had to be live at the Chase, I had to be in St. Louis if I wanted to be a star."

—**Ric Flair**

Ali Baba and George Zaharias

PREFACE

IT BEGAN AS A CONVERSATION between two men on an airplane, and it turned into a near 25-year love affair spanning multiple generations of fans across mid-America. *Wrestling at the Chase's* 1959 premiere fueled a phenomenon. It started a trend that drew hundreds of men and women dressed to the nines ringside each week in the Khorassan Room of the opulent Chase Park Plaza Hotel sitting on the northeast edge of St. Louis's historic Forest Park. At the same time all across the Midwest, as the clock struck 9 o'clock each Saturday evening, hundreds of thousands more turned their television sets to the newest station in town, KPLR Channel 11, to watch the show. They sat in the comfort of their living rooms eating popcorn and drinking soda, feeling just like those swells of society all dressed up ringside. A new audience of thousands more tuned in to Channel 11 once more the next morning as the show and action was re-aired every Sunday morning.

This book is a tribute to Sam Muchnick and Harold Koplar, two men on a plane ride who created their own successful ride of a lifetime with this innovative program. It is also a tribute to so many others who touched *Wrestling at the Chase* in so many ways. Some were big names in St. Louis and its sports history, like the Garagiola brothers, Joe and Mickey. Others made their names in the program as ringside announcers. Then there were the wrestlers themselves with the monikers of Bruiser, Gorgeous George, Honest Johnny, King Kong, and Nature Boy to name just a few. There was Larry Matysik, a man who continued to carry the torch and kept the show and action going in the later years of the program. Finally there's Herb Simmons, Larry's partner and friend who has taken that torch today so that the light continues to shine on one of the most beloved and iconic programs in St. Louis sports history. This is the story of *Wrestling at the Chase* and how the three legs of the stool (the location, the delivery, and the product) came together to support nearly three decades of entertainment across Middle America and create countless memories for generations beyond.

Dick the Bruiser corners Black Jack Lanza.

The voice of the fan— Mickey Garagiola
COURTESY OF BOB GARAGIOLA

Pat O'Connor tangles
with Lou Thesz.

PART 1

THE THREE LEGS OF THE STOOL COME TOGETHER

Buddy Rogers won the 1961 world championship from Pat O'Connor (*right*).

Johnny Valentine

IN THE BEGINNING

THE SPORT OF WRESTLING precedes *Wrestling at the Chase* matches by thousands of years. Considered by many to be the oldest competitive sport, it can be traced back to the beginning of mankind where it initially evolved as one of the oldest forms of combat. Representations of wrestling have been found in cave drawings of prehistoric man dating back to 3000 BC, as well as in the artistic reliefs and other artwork of ancient Egypt, Babylonia, and other civilizations of the Middle East. It can be found across the Orient as well and in the emerging civilizations of Europe. Shuai jiao is a form of wrestling in China that spans a history of over 4,000 years. In Arabic cultures, stories highlight the prophet Muhammad as a skilled wrestler defeating a skeptic champion in a noted match. Wrestling is even called out in the Bible's book of Genesis (32:24): "And Jacob was left alone; and there wrestled a man with him until the breaking of the day." But it was the Greeks and then the Romans who brought wrestling to the forefront with mythological exploits told in the tales of the rise of Zeus or the fabled matches of Heracles against man and beast. It is from these two early Mediterranean cultures that wrestling became one of the founding pillars of the ancient Olympic Games. In 708 BC, wrestling was the first competition added to the Olympic Games

Wrestlers take center stage on an ancient Greek relief of the pentathlon, 500 BC.
COURTESY OF WIKIMEDIA COMMONS

that was not a footrace. It was also a part of the evolution of the modern Olympic Games held in Athens, Greece, in 1896, and it has continued as a fixture in every Olympic Games since.

Greco-Roman wrestling remains a part of the Olympic Games today, with competitors only allowed to use their arms and upper bodies to attack. It is a style that pays homage to the purest form of wrestling from those ancient Games. But in the 1904 Olympic Games—held, ironically, in St. Louis—participants competed in the freestyle format for the first time. This form of wrestling would evolve into the competitive style used by combatants during their *Wrestling at the Chase* matches. Unlike Greco-Roman, freestyle wrestling allows the use of the wrestler's or the opponent's legs

Wrestling scenes found in Egypt's Beni Hasan tomb.
COURTESY OF WIKIMEDIA COMMONS

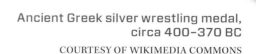

Ancient Greek silver wrestling medal, circa 400–370 BC
COURTESY OF WIKIMEDIA COMMONS

in offense and defense. Freestyle wrestling brings together traditional wrestling, judo, and sambo techniques.

But wrestling has not been just an Olympic sport. It has a long history in the United States. Its popularity grew as the nation expanded through the 19th century into the 20th century. Like all professional sports today, wrestling began with amateur competitions. It flourished as a popular form of competition and entertainment at fairs and other public events before there were movie theaters, television, or video games. During these times, matches were true battles of strength, athleticism, and conquest. It was a legitimate sport, and that legitimacy remains intact today, not only in the Olympics but in high school and college matches across the United States and the globe.

Contestants wrestling at the 1904 Olympics in St. Louis.
COURTESY OF WIKIMEDIA COMMONS

MAT MOMENTS

HOW COINCIDENTAL IS IT THAT the Chase Park Plaza Hotel sits adjacent to Forest Park, where some of the 1904 Olympic Games' activities were held? The Olympic wrestling matches took place on the infield of the Olympic Stadium at Francis Field, which still stands on the Washington University campus at the west end of Forest Park.

WRESTLING TAKES A TURN

DURING THE 1920S, there was an offshoot of professional wrestling that was becoming more theatric in nature with an admitted amount of staged performance that moved the sport more toward entertainment and further away from true competition. Although remaining very physical, it was becoming athletic theater. That is not to say that there was no athleticism, strength, or guile in this wrestling format, but the performances were now choreographed rather than competitive. And people, in their naivety, loved it. Simply put, it had become an exciting form of entertainment that would attain a national cult status that continues today.

Within this entertaining world of professional wrestling there evolved the term "kayfabe" (pronounced /kā fāb/), which describes the portrayal of staged events (in this case wrestling) as real competitions between combatants before the general public. It was necessary to ensure that the staged portrayal of competition between wrestling foes was maintained in order to promote the sense of reality and suspense among the audience. While the scripted nature of these professional wrestling matches was largely an open secret, it was generally neither promoted or openly acknowledged by those in the business. In fact, wrestlers and promoters went to extremes to ensure that ring adversaries would not be seen publicly or photographed together socializing in order to maintain the impression that the rivalries were real.

MAT MOMENTS

IT WAS ALMOST LIKE BEING TOLD THERE'S NO SANTA CLAUS. Newspaper columnist Joe Holleman remembers the time when he was around 11 or 12 and his dad broke the news that the wrestling he loved to watch every Saturday night wasn't really what he thought it was. Joe's dad was a truck driver who made deliveries to the Chase Park Plaza Hotel. One day while his truck was being unloaded, his dad went inside to grab some lunch. To his surprise, also sitting in the restaurant were Dick the Bruiser, Fritz Von Erich, and Bob Geigel, who went by the nickname "the Hairy Ape." In the crowded dining room, the grapplers simply looked like three regular (but large) guys just sharing a lunch table. But to a wrestling fan like Joe's dad, they were legends, and he couldn't wait to get home to tell young Joe.

As his dad began explaining his lunchtime experience, Joe became perplexed. His head was full of questions. "Why were these men sitting and eating together? They were mortal enemies in the ring. They just couldn't be at the same table laughing and eating like best friends!" In disbelief, Joe asked, "What's going on?" So Joe's dad sat him down and explained the nature of professional wrestling. For a week or two, young Joe was hurt. The action on the small screen the next few Saturday nights just didn't seem quite the same. But like so many other things in life, the feeling didn't last long. Joe realized there was much more to his Saturday night entertainment, and he soon was back in front of the television set rooting and screaming at his favorite program.

Bob Geigel, a.k.a. "the Hairy Ape"

Dick the Bruiser

To the believing public, the action was real beyond any doubt. To so many diehard fans, there was nothing fake about the athleticism and acrobatics of these athletes and the violence they inflicted, be it a head slam into the turnbuckles of the ropes or a crushing fist blow to the head. A body slam is still a body slam that jars a wrestler's insides and twists his spine. Sure, there were times when a match went off script, most likely when a wrestler became injured, but the unspoken agreement to treat the events inside the ring as reality remained sacred and unbroken. Just like the residents of the Emerald City in *The Wizard of Oz*, most wrestling fans did not want to know—and did not care—what was happening behind the curtain. That was the mystique of professional wrestling, and it brought people back week after week through wrestling's golden decades of the 1950s and 1960s. And there was no better place to grab a seat than the gilded Khorassan Room of the Chase Park Plaza Hotel.

MAT MOMENTS

IT HAD TO BE REAL—RIGHT? Or so it seemed. Countless stories have been told across the Midwest of adolescent viewers of *Wrestling at the Chase* mirroring the unknowing kayfabe moves of their favorite grapplers. Body slams threw siblings across living room tables as imitated wrestling holds and moves crushed furniture and dented walls. To the regret of so many parents, the transition from the television screen to their home was not staged and controlled action. It was real, and it was damaging. But boy, oh boy, was it fun, and what a memory!

Fritz Von Erich prepares to throw Buddy Marino to the mat.
COURTESY OF GETTY IMAGES

A VENUE FIT FOR ROYALTY

THE HOTEL CHASE, as it was initially called, was the most luxurious hotel in St. Louis right from its opening in 1922. At the time of its construction, St. Louis was a burgeoning city, the sixth largest in the nation, and the new hotel was christened "'the miracle hotel of the miracle city', swathed in elegance and grandeur. For years it was the focal point of glamour and entertainment in St. Louis."[1]

Located in the city's Central West End, the nine-story hotel sits at the northeast corner of St. Louis's historic Forest Park at the intersection of Kingshighway and Lindell Boulevards. The Chase's setting was reminiscent of the grand New York hotels and the stunning apartment buildings sitting along the avenues of that city's famed Central Park. In St. Louis, the Chase sits surrounded by large mansions built just before and after one of St. Louis's golden moments—the 1904 World's Fair—which had taken place across the street in Forest Park. Besides a hotel, the Chase was known nationally through the years as one of the premier nightclubs in the United States with its cabaret, the Chase Club, headlining the country's top performers and entertainers.

The Chase Hotel
COURTESY OF WIKIPEDIA

Nat King Cole performs in the Chase Club.

COURTESY OF SAM KOPLAR

FRANK SINATRA

IN SAINT LOUIS

The Chase is the Place

Only the best performed or stayed at the Chase Hotel.

COURTESY OF THE AUTHOR

It's where presidents, kings and queens, movie stars, and major league ballplayers stayed when their shows or teams came to town. The Chase hosted just about anyone who was anyone who came to St. Louis as well as most of the city's high-society events. "Stars including Tony Bennett, Jimmy Durante, Sophie Tucker, and Nat King Cole performed there, as did the big bands of Guy Lombardo and Stan Kenton. Presidents from Franklin D. Roosevelt to Gerald Ford stayed there."[2] The Chase was simply the place to be!

During the 1920s, St. Louisan Sam Koplar had begun with a brick salvaging business and eventually built a real estate empire that developed some of the city's most fashionable and recognizable buildings. The Embassy Apartments at Union and Washington and the twin Congress Hotel and Senate Apartments complex on the northern edge of Forest Park at Union Boulevard are just a few of Koplar's developments that dotted the St. Louis skyline. One

Sam Koplar
COURTESY OF MERCANTILE LIBRARY

particularly iconic example in Koplar's portfolio was the St. Louis Theatre, built in 1925 at the intersection of Grand Avenue and Delmar Boulevard. Initially built as a vaudeville palace, it transitioned with the advent of motion pictures to one of the city's premier movie theaters before being remodeled to become Powell Hall, today's home of the St. Louis Symphony. Sam Koplar was leaving his mark across St. Louis as a leader in development and in the community.

In 1929, Sam Koplar began building the gem of this empire: the Park Plaza Hotel, a 28-story tower modeled after New York's elegant

The Congress and Senate buildings
COURTESY OF SAM KOPLAR

The St. Louis Theatre
COURTESY OF MISSOURI HISTORICAL SOCIETY

Savoy Plaza Hotel, on a parcel of land adjacent to the north side of the Chase Hotel. His new hotel's name was derived from Park (from Forest Park) and Plaza (from the Savoy Plaza).[3] Even though Koplar would temporarily lose the Park Plaza to foreclosure during the Great Depression, he continued to work as a desk manager, determined to reacquire his "baby." By the mid-1940s, it was his again (for $3 million, about half the $6 million it cost to build). And he didn't get just the Park Plaza; he was soon able to take over ownership of the neighboring Chase Hotel as well. Over time the buildings' operations and names would merge, and it became simply the Chase Park Plaza. The Koplar family, with their flagship property in place, was well positioned to become a key player in what would become the saga of *Wrestling at the Chase*.

The Park Plaza under construction
COURTESY OF SAM KOPLAR

The Park Plaza became Koplar's Chase and Park Plaza.
MISSOURI HISTORICAL SOCIETY

THEATER ON A WRESTLING MAT

WHILE THE KOPLAR FAMILY was building their empire between 1920 and 1960, wrestling's popularity was growing by leaps and bounds. Wrestling had evolved and flourished as a legitimate and competitive sport for thousands of years until roughly the early 1920s. While truly tests of strength and agility, these matches were actually slow-moving exhibitions confined to the mat itself, and a single bout could last well over an hour. During the Roaring Twenties, the pace of American society was picking up, and the fans no longer found these matches entertaining. Traveling carnival shows and vaudeville halls helped stimulate what would become the staged entertainment of professional wrestling. Although change was in the air, authentic matches would continue to be wrestled over the next several decades, but outside schools and the Olympics they would become increasingly rare. A whole new world of professional wrestling was advancing.

The sport was undergoing a transformation. This new era of professional wrestling was increasingly built around dramatic

Wrestling

Collectible wrestling tobacco card, 1925
COURTESY OF GETTY IMAGES

MAT MOMENTS

IN A DECEMBER 1953 ARTICLE, *St. Louis Post-Dispatch* sports columnist John Wray sought to explain "Why Do People Look at Wrestling Bouts?" He noted that "what they do on the mat today is 'rassle,' not wrestle in our opinion—expressed for a quarter of a century in this column. Not that we have anything against acrobatics, vaudeville or comedy. . . . But there is a certain distinction between the real and the simulated. . . ." Changes were taking place in wrestling because people wanted action and drama added to the matches, no matter what the means. They didn't want the stale days of yore. Wray's column recalled a mat event that took place at the South Broadway Athletic Club nearly 50 years ago, between Mike Christ and Freddie Doerr, "It started in the afternoon. . . . Club members went home to supper but the wrestlers were still at it when the members came back. It was five hours after the start that Doerr finally won."

COURTESY OF THE AUTHOR

Wrestling magazines added to the drama and larger-than-life adventures of professional wrestling.

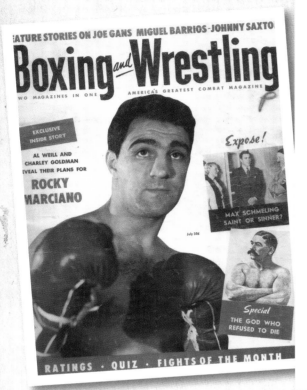

COURTESY OF THE AUTHOR

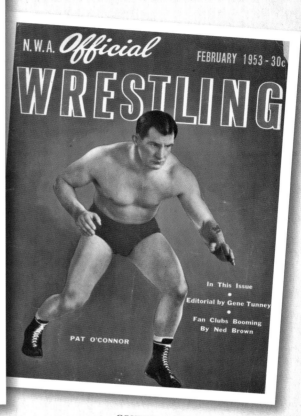

COURTESY OF BOB GARAGIOLA

individual personalities and staged feuds as part of the buildup and promotion of upcoming matches. While big in physical stature, the wrestlers themselves evolved into larger-than-life characters in what became the stage-managed drama of professional wrestling. Individual wrestlers began developing identities that were becoming just as scripted as the matches themselves. These wrestlers were truly strong and healthy athletes whose stage had turned from near mortal physical combat to theater on a wrestling mat, and it seemed to suit them and their fans well. These planned and choreographed matches required precise execution but were less taxing physically. The controlled environment also meant less risk of injury, so the wrestlers could compete in four or five matches across the country each week, resulting in more payoffs to promoters and their warriors.

The general public loved the athleticism, acrobatics, speed, and feats of strength these matches brought to the fans ringside. Professional wrestling's success was soon paired with the evolving trade magazines of the time, each ripe with storylines of individual wrestlers' inflated egos and personal melodrama. Furthermore, and unlike today, St. Louis newspapers from the 1940s through the late 1960s regularly filled their sports sections with banner headlines, photos, and descriptions of professional wrestling matches held at the Arena, Kiel Auditorium, and other venues across town. Sportswriters like Ray Gillespie, Bob Broeg, Bob Burnes, and Keith Schildroth regularly brought the excitement of professional wrestling to daily readers.

As Larry Matysik tells it, beginning in the 1930s all the way until the 1970s, Kiel Auditorium was the capital of wrestling in the United States.[4] Led first by wrestling promoters Tom Packs and then Sam Muchnick, the auditorium held around eighteen events filled to the rafters every year. It was a great place for the ten thousand plus fans to watch wrestling up close. On their way to the ring for each match, wrestlers entered from the stage at the rear of the auditorium and walked down a long aisle right through the middle of the crowd.

Upon seeing the grappler begin his march, the audience erupted with loud shrieking screams while also stomping their feet to create one of the loudest wrestling venues in the nation. It was so easy for the unknowing fans filling Kiel and other arenas shrouded by the veil of the kayfabe to be lost in the drama of it all, even if it was all scripted and predetermined. Fans attended by the thousands because it was such great entertainment and they loved it!

The legendary Kiel Auditorium located at 14th and Market Streets
COURTESY OF THE AUTHOR

THE MAN WHO MADE WRESTLING A REAL SPORT

COWBOY LUTTRALL
TAMPA, FL

JIM CROCKETT
CHARLOTTE, NC

THE WORLD'S TOP WRESTLING PROMOTERS

IT ALL SEEMED to be a win-win situation that had the opportunity to yield bigger rewards. These matches soon became the instruments of regional promoters—men and organizations that spawned across the country. During these early years, professional wrestling was essentially an independent collection of regional promoters with their own "world champions."

These syndicates were limited to matches strictly within their own geographic boundaries under the purview of the National Wrestling Association.[5]

VINCE MCMAHON, SR.
WASHINGTON, DC

SAM MUCHNICK
ST. LOUIS, MO

FRED KOHLER
CHICAGO, IL

MORRIS SIEGAL
HOUSTON, TX

TOOTS MONDT
PITTSBURGH, PA

FRANK TUNNEY
TORONTO, CANADA

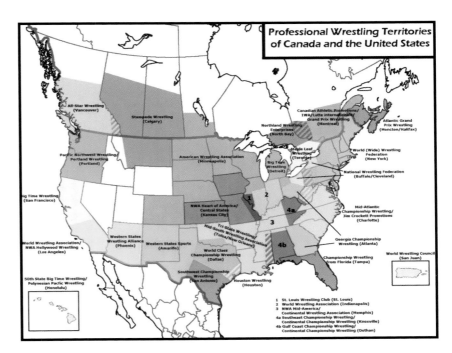

WIKIMEDIA COMMONS. ATTRIBUTION: KYLE KUSCH, THE BASEMENT GEOGRAPHER.

The association, which had spun off of the National Boxing Association in September 1930, was not always pretty. It was basically a dirty business that one man from St. Louis more than anyone else turned into a real sport. That man was Sam Muchnick. He would become the greatest wrestling promoter of the St. Louis area. His tentacles would reach across the nation, and he would eventually be recognized as one of the true leaders of wrestling entertainment nationwide.

Sam Muchnick

SAM MUCHNICK

MAT MOMENTS

ED LEWIS, BILLY SANDOW, AND TOOTS MONDT were three professional wrestlers who helped lead this transition of wrestling and its promotion in the 1920s. The three joined forces and formed their own promotions operation to enhance the action in the ring and the appeal to adoring fans. They eventually earned the moniker the "Gold Dust Trio" due to their success. They set a new paradigm for their matches. They were the first to introduce time-limit matches. They evolved flashy new "holds" and "counters" while developing signature maneuvers trademarked for given wrestlers.[6] To add to the excitement, they also popularized tag-team wrestling. Their shtick added vaudevillian tactics to enhance the audience's entertainment and fun with such tricks as distracting the referee so that "illegal" moves and other rule breaking would go unpunished. And to make this all work and keep their programs under control, they began keeping wrestlers under contract for years at a time. They became their wrestlers' brokers and agents in order to maintain their storylines and appeal. The success of these efforts soon had them firmly in control of wrestling in North America.

Toots Mondt

Ed "Strangle" Lewis

TOP: COURTESY OF MARK KERN
BOTTOM: COURTESY OF WIKIMEDIA COMMONS

Sam Muchnick's career during the golden years of the sport of wrestling draws many comparisons to Pete Rozelle bringing the National Football League to prominence. Each was a forward thinker who revolutionized his particular sport. The Ukrainian-born Muchnick had come to the United States in 1912 and shortly thereafter moved to St. Louis, growing up in the Kerry Patch community located around 14th and Franklin (Martin Luther King Jr. Drive today) Streets on the city's north side. After graduating from Central High School, Muchnick worked as a postal worker and then a newspaper reporter for the *St. Louis Times* covering the St. Louis Cardinals baseball team through four World Series appearances, as well as the city's wrestling scene in the 1920s and 1930s. He was

THOMAS N. PACKS ENTERPRISES
280-284 Arcade Bldg., ST. LOUIS 1, MO.

THESZ vs. LONGSON
KIEL AUD. — NOV. 21st

A Tom Packs promotion

Promoter Tom Packs and his wrestlers Bill Longson (*left*) and Lou Thesz (*right*)

a man on the move, and through his sports coverage he made the acquaintance of movers and shakers from Babe Ruth to Al Capone.

Soon Muchnick was on the move again, aligning with one of the region's top wrestling promoters, Tom Packs. Packs hired Sam when the *Times* folded in 1932 after its merger with the *St. Louis Star* newspaper. Packs liked Sam's professionalism in reporting. It enhanced wrestling's style and legitimacy. Muchnick became a jack of all trades in Packs's operations,

ST. LOUIS WRESTLING CLUB, INC.
SAM MUCHNICK SPORTS ATTRACTION
NATIONAL WRESTLING ALLIANCE
OFFICE HOURS - 10 A.M. to 3:30 P.M.

• Special Courtesy Card •

1950 Wrestling Season — Good Until Jan. 1, 1951

This card Name_____
entitles Address_____

To purchase one or more reserved seat tickets in special sections of ringside or mezzanine WHILE AVAILABLE for wrestling events under the promotion of Sam Muchnick Sports Attractions at 75 cents per ticket. These tickets must be obtained not later than 5 p.m. date of attractions at ADAM HAT STORE box office, 710 Olive St., St. Louis, Mo.

(No Telephone Reservations Taken on These Tickets)

(Over)   SAM MUCHNICK, Promoter

After the Fights — Meet the Crowd at the Newest and Smartest Night Club in St. Louis
ULTRA MODERN IN DESIGN — THE FINEST IN ENTERTAINMENT

THE NEW

CLUB PLANTATION

3617 DELMAR

Presenting an all New York Show — 49 People

UNDER DIRECTION OF LEONARD REED
DIRECT FROM THE COTTON CLUB — NEW YORK

● RHUMBA NIGHT EVERY WEDNESDAY ●

JETER-PILLARS RECORDING ORCHESTRA

SAME PRICE POLICY   Sponsored by TONY SCARPEI

(Formerly Palladium Roller Rink)

CLUB PLANTATION

SALUTES

THE ALL-STAR WRESTLING PROGRAM

★ ★ ★

UNDER THE DIRECTION OF

TOM PACKS

★ ★ ★

TUESDAY, OCTOBER 29th
8:15 P. M.

Municipal Auditorium

Marvel Ptg. Co., 912 N. Seventh St.

COURTESY OF MARK KERN   COURTESY OF MARK KERN

working public relations and finances and eventually handling event bookings. Most importantly, Sam was learning all aspects of wrestling operations. After nine years, the relationship soured over the amount of a bonus payment Sam expected from a very profitable Joe Louis heavyweight title bout in April 1941 that Muchnick helped Packs promote. Buoyed by other wrestlers and promoters who were also becoming disgruntled with the powerful Packs, Muchnick went his own way and began putting together his very own promotions under the Sam Muchnick Sports Attractions banner. His first show was in St. Louis's Kiel Auditorium on December 5, 1945. Eventually Sam Muchnick Sports Attractions would be renamed the St. Louis Wrestling Club.

During their breakup, Muchnick and Packs remained at odds, with Sam limited to second-class matches starring lesser talent. Packs had the sport's top stars, including world champion Lou Thesz, in

his ring. Even with Packs continually throwing his weight around in the grappling industry and making it hard for Muchnick to promote attractive programs, the feud between the two parties did have one payoff: it regularly brought great matches to St. Louis, to the enjoyment of a growing fan base. Packs's tactics nearly worked, as Muchnick's operations operated in the red during those initial years. Muchnick told the *Post-Dispatch* on May 30, 1948, "Well I finally did it. After three years of battling, this is the first year I have finished out of the red. In fact, this season I have made a very comfortable living. I lost money my first two seasons. But my attendances during most of the year were well in the black. I've slowly been forging ahead and feel I now have a permanency." Always regarded as an honest promoter, Muchnick continued to work hard and build relationships as he pushed forward.

MAT
MOMENTS

TOM PACKS WAS A GREEK immigrant who crisscrossed the United States learning the art of wrestling promotions from New York to Chicago before settling in St. Louis during the early 1920s and turning his new hometown into one of the top wrestling territories in the nation. He built a stable of big-name grapplers led by Bill Longson, Abe Coleman, Orville Brown, and Fred Blassie that turned him into arguably the industry's most powerful promoter. Packs's power in the National Wrestling Association grew further as he fostered and controlled the career of one of the greatest champions of all time, Lou Thesz.

Orville Brown

Wild Bill Longson

Lou Thesz

Then things began to change for the good in 1948. Muchnick's hard work and a little good luck began to pay off. Packs started running into financial difficulties of his own doing. A litany of poor investments in the stock market had caught up to him, and he chose to close his wrestling enterprise. He sold Tom Packs Sport Enterprises to the Mississippi Valley Sports Club, which was a group led by his star wrestler Lou Thesz. Unknown to nearly everyone, Sam held a 50 percent control in Thesz's venture and was thus calling the shots in both wrestling organizations. It was a shrewd move that kept both promotions alive.[7] Packs had given young Sam his start in the wrestling promotion game, and with his departure Muchnick was left with a town that had been transformed into the heart of the professional wrestling world.

During this same period, Muchnick was approached by Iowa promoter Pinkie George and Minnesota's Tony Stecher about creating a coalition of promoters representing the various wrestling commissions around the country, to be called the National Wrestling Alliance (NWA). Up until that time, these commissions had been guided by men like Tom Packs under the controlling arm of the National Wrestling Association, which completely oversaw all pro wrestling regulations.

CHAMPIONSHIP WRESTLING

MAIN EVENT
One Fall to A Finish

Friday Night, Sept. 24, '48

ENRIQUE TORRES
(Mexican Mat Sensation)
(Conqueror of Wild Bill Longson)
— vs. —
LOU THESZ
(N.W.A. Champion)

—— SEMI-FINAL ——
KILLER CARL DAVIS
— vs. —
AL LOVELOCK

Australian Team Match
SEE THE ZAHARIAS BOYS!
— vs. —
MICKEY GOLD and JOE MILLICH
RAY GUNKLE vs. JOE DUSEK

SPORTS POINTERS will be sent to you on request. Send us your name and address, along with $1.00 for one year's subscription.

MISSISSIPPI VALLEY SPORTS CLUB
280 Arcade Bldg., St. Louis, Mo.

Mississippi Valley Sports Club promotion

The new alliance assigned each member promoter a defined geographic territory. With that structure in place, this new alliance would do things differently. They would share the bookings of the top wrestlers as well as the alliance's sole crowned world champion. Within the alliance, there would be movement of wrestlers between territories to ensure that fans never tired of a wrestler. A wrestler could move to a new territory as a fresh new star to a new crowd of fans. For the big payoffs, the NWA world champion did not have a home territory but instead would travel and defend his title against the top wrestlers of each territory. It was agreed that Orville Brown would become the first world heavyweight champion of the alliance. These actions would ensure financial success for each promoter while preserving each territory's revenue stream. On July 19, 1948, this group of promoters met and formalized the National Wrestling Alliance in Waterloo, Iowa.

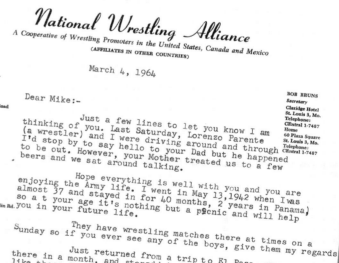

BRIAN WALSH

Pinkie George
COURTESY OF WIKIMEDIA COMMONS

Tony Stecher

While Pinkie George was named the organization's first president, Muchnick had an immediate payoff. Not only did the gate sharing help financially, but the talent-sharing arrangement brought wrestlers to Muchnick's operations that he hadn't been able to get during his rivalry with Packs. Things were picking up, and on February 4, 1949, a Sam Muchnick–promoted wrestling program would have its first sellout at St. Louis's Kiel Auditorium. That match featured a new grappler whom Muchnick had added to his wrestling promotions—Buddy Rogers, a.k.a. "Nature Boy." Rogers battled Chief Don Eagle in that night's match and brought immediate charisma and legitimacy to Muchnick's promotions. From that point forward, things continued to pick up for Sam and his team.

Don Eagle
COURTESY OF WIKIMEDIA COMMONS

Buddy Rogers

Sam Muchnick signing Buddy Rogers to his team

MAT MOMENTS

BESIDES BEING A MAKER OF CHAMPIONS, Sam Muchnick may have been, in a way, a maker of presidents as well. During the waning days of the hard-fought 1948 presidential race between Harry Truman and Thomas Dewey, Truman needed an important event to be held for his campaign in St. Louis. Kiel Auditorium was the logical site. The problem was that Sam already had a big wrestling event scheduled there on the night in question. When asked to free up the venue, the wrestling promoter thought about it for a while and replied, "Well I got a show, but for the president, I'll change it." The rest is history. Against predictions, the underdog Truman won a very close election. While returning to Washington two days after the election from his home in Independence, Missouri, the newly reelected president's train stopped in St. Louis Union Station. While celebrating before a large crowd from the back of his railcar, Mr. Truman was handed the *Chicago Daily*

Tribune newspaper from the previous day with the famous headline "Dewey Defeats Truman," which the president held high before the crowd in jest. That moment was captured in one of presidential history's greatest photos. Perhaps Sam Muchnick's generosity helped make that famous headline one of history's biggest mistakes.

THE WHITE HOUSE
WASHINGTON

September 10, 1948

Dear Sam:

John Nangle has just informed me of your generosity with regard to the Auditorium for Friday, October twenty-ninth. I can't tell you how very much I appreciate your courtesy in this matter.

I hope to see you that evening.

Sincerely yours,

Harry Truman

Sam Muchnick
Locust Street
t Louis 3, Missouri

Truman's thank-you to Sam for his generosity and perhaps presidency
COURTESY OF
KATHY MUCHNICK SCHNIEDER

Chicago Daily Tribune — Home
DEWEY DEFEATS TRUMAN
G.O.P. Sweep Indicated in State; Boyle Leads in City

Dewey defeats Truman
COURTESY OF GETTY IMAGES

SAM MUCHNICK SPORTS ATTRACTIONS

WRESTLING

DON EAGLE VS. BUDDY ROGERS

KIEL AUDITORIUM   ST. LOUIS, MO.   FEB. 4, 1949

PHOTOGRAPH BY EUGENE TAYLOR

22

Lou Thesz in the meantime had begun taking over Tom Packs's operations in the competing National Wrestling Association. Thesz initially refused Muchnick's offer to merge the companies, but after the success of Muchnick's promotions the two groups from St. Louis finally merged as one in November 1949. Shortly after that union, Thesz became the consolidated National Wrestling Alliance heavyweight champion when the incumbent champion, Orville Brown, was injured in an automobile accident that would end his career. The world of professional wrestling was changing for the better, and most of that was due to Sam Muchnick. He was clearly the right guy at the right time. The sport still had many promoters who operated matches like they were in traveling carnivals or vaudeville. But Muchnick, who had been baptized in the sports world during his newspaper reporting days, was transforming professional wrestling into a credible business and an entertaining sport.

World champion
Lou Thesz
COURTESY OF GETTY IMAGES

Sam and Lou
coming to terms

The championship
match that never happened

MAT MOMENTS

WHEN TALKING WITH WRESTLERS AND MEMBERS of the press from Muchnick's era, the same few words recur in each conversation: "fair and respected." Bill Apter, a longtime wrestling photographer and columnist, said "he looked like an executive and would command respect without asking for it." He added, "Although he was the king of an amazing empire, he treated me as an equal even the first time I met him." Wrestler Baron Von Raschke said, "He treated the wrestlers with respect and hired good bookers and listened to their advice. He loved the fans."

Bill Apter on his induction into the St. Louis Wrestling Hall of Fame

As the clock struck midnight and a new decade was born in 1950, Sam Muchnick was named the new president of the National Wrestling Alliance, and professional wrestling entered its golden years. Sam had made it to the top and was there to stay. He would take professional wrestling to a new level that would bring nearly two decades of stability in what had been at times an underhanded profession. The trust and respect Muchnick had earned across professional wrestling were reflected in the nine straight unanimous elections that kept him at the top each year. Sam was now presiding over the dominant governing body in professional wrestling, with its financial wealth and stable of top talent. Muchnick served as the organization's president through 1960 and then filled the position again from 1963 to 1975. During this time, *Wrestling Review* magazine declared Muchnick the most prominent man in professional wrestling. During his second tour as leader of the organization, he not only brought calm and profitability but also expanded operations outside the United States into Europe, Japan, Mexico, and other Caribbean countries. With Sam at the helm, the eyes of the wrestling

SAM MUCHNICK: FAIR AND RESPECTED

world remained focused on St. Louis. His lineup of top talent and world champions would be regulars in the river city. Wrestler Cowboy Bob Orton, whose father, Bob Sr., appeared on the very first episode of *Wrestling at the Chase,* summed up the situation very well: "Everyone wanted to work St. Louis. It was said if you made it to St Louis with Sam, you made it to the big times."

Bob Orton Sr.

Ted Koplar
COURTESY OF ST. LOUIS MEDIA
HISTORY FOUNDATION

As Ted Koplar (the son of the Chase Park Plaza Hotel and KPLR-TV owner Harold Koplar), who would one day become owner of the station and occasional director of *Wrestling at the Chase,* noted:

"Muchnick does not receive the recognition today that he deserves. He was Mr. Wrestling. Sam made the whole phenomenon happen. It was born here [St. Louis]; it was bred here . . . and if this town had never accepted it the way it did, wrestling might never have become a national success. Sam was recognized nationally. He was the Vince McMahon of his day—around the world."[8]

ST. LOUIS WRESTLING CLUB, INC.

(Headquarters - Telephone: 361-6855)
CHASE-PARK PLAZA HOTEL, 3255-56
212 No. Kingshighway
St. Louis, Mo. 63108

Featuring World's Greatest Wrestlers

TICKET OFFICE Mezzanine 10 - Arcade Building
812 Olive Street - St. Louis, Mo. 63101
TELEPHONE: 436-4400
Information, 24 Hours a day: 361-6870

Sam was the man. Pat Matysik, wife of Muchnick's longtime protégé Larry Matysik, had a front-row seat observing their success. She recalled Sam this way:

"Sam and by extension Larry were part of the fabric of the community. No promoter anywhere in the country enjoyed such an intimate relationship with his town like Sam did. This was something other promoters failed to understand. The way Sam conducted a notorious endeavor like professional wrestling in and out of the ring was unique, and all the little touches added up and mattered. Sam Muchnick was respected by all the levels of society. He was conscious of how some people had a negative view of professional wrestling, and he always tried to rise above that view by being scrupulously honest, fair, and unbiased."

The St. Louis Wrestling Club was Sam's local organization under the National Wrestling Alliance. It was one of the 32 territorial wrestling promotions organizations formed under the National Wrestling Alliance. Not only did the St. Louis club rise to prominence, its star shone even brighter due to Muchnick's national leadership and the club's association with what would become one of the most iconic programs in the history of professional wrestling—*Wrestling at the Chase*. Just as the National Wrestling Alliance flourished under Muchnick's oversight, so too did the St. Louis Wrestling Club. But it was the marriage of Muchnick's wrestling enterprise product and television that changed everything.

MAT
MOMENTS

BEFORE THERE WAS WRESTLING ON television in St. Louis, there was big-time wrestling that came to town thanks to Sam's operations. Muchnick's promotions were like a magnet attracting the best wrestlers to the river city. Over ten thousand screaming fans would be packed to the rafters of the St. Louis Arena or Kiel Auditorium. If it were not for Sam's early successes and promotions at these venues, *Wrestling at the Chase* never would have hit the airwaves and been a decades-long success. Even when the television program rose to the peak of its success, the real money in St. Louis wrestling still came from the wrestling cards promoted at these two locations. Televised wrestling was really just a break-even proposition. Big venues with big audiences were needed to turn a profit. Unlike promoters in most towns, Sam Muchnick didn't have to pay to air his product on television. In fact, KPLR-TV paid the St. Louis Wrestling Club $1,500 per taping day in return for 5 percent of the net receipts from each Kiel Auditorium and Arena card.[9] Here in St. Louis it was special, and it worked. It was a great product that attracted fans and wrestlers together for that one special time slot every Saturday night.

The St. Louis Arena
in the 1940s
COURTESY OF MISSOURI
HISTORICAL SOCIETY

TELEVISION BRINGS WRESTLING TO THE MASSES

SAM MUCHNICK, however, was not the first to bring professional wrestling to either St. Louis or the nation's television airwaves. During the infancy of television, the long-forgotten DuMont Television Network aired wrestling matches nationwide from Chicago, Illinois, on Saturday nights. The program was called *Wrestling from Marigold*, and it aired from September 1949 to March 1955. Chicago's WGN-TV then broadcast the program for another two years. The title is derived from the location of the matches, the Marigold Arena on Chicago's north side. It was produced by Chicago's National Wrestling Alliance promoter, Fred Kohler. *Wrestling from Marigold* was initially televised in St. Louis on the city's first television station, KSD-TV. The station first signed on the air on February 8, 1947, as the 13th television station in the country.[10]

COURTESY OF WIKIMEDIA COMMONS

Although KSD-TV was an NBC affiliate, it also filled its programming with other network-produced shows. The station initially aired the wrestling program on Saturday nights at 9:30 p.m. The next year, it also televised additional wrestling matches from Chicago's International Amphitheatre on Wednesday nights at 8 p.m.

COURTESY OF WIKIMEDIA COMMONS

MAT
MOMENTS

In 1953, *Wrestling from Marigold* moved to WTVI-54, a UHF (ultra high frequency) station in Belleville, Illinois, located about six miles east of downtown St. Louis. WTVI was the region's second operating television station when it debuted on August 10, 1953, airing DuMont network programming and locally produced shows. During the early years of television, the DuMont network was a major national player on the same level as ABC, CBS, and NBC. Once the DuMont network ceased operations in 1956, WTVI became KTVI-2 as an ABC affiliate before becoming the Fox Network's St. Louis affiliate in 1995.

Muchnick initially liked the idea of televised wrestling shown from afar, because those matches helped promote interest in the

WTVI advertisement promoting wrestling
COURTESY OF ST. LOUIS MEDIA HISTORY FOUNDATION

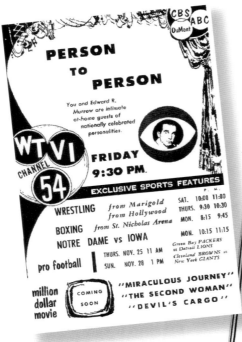

Although promoting an on-air date of May, the station did not hit the airwaves until August.
COURTESY OF ST. LOUIS MEDIA HISTORY FOUNDATION

Television station WTVI in Belleville, Illinois
COURTESY OF ST. LOUIS MEDIA HISTORY FOUNDATION

MAT MOMENTS

WTVI'S VERY FIRST PROGRAM, shown in 1953, was a benefit baseball game between the American League St. Louis Browns and the National League Cincinnati Reds from the newly named Busch Stadium (formerly Sportsman's Park). The game was called by announcers Buddy Blattner and Dizzy Dean. The station had completed a deal to carry Browns games on a regular basis, and the second day's programming schedule consisted of a doubleheader between the Browns and the Detroit Tigers. There was a 15-minute newscast between games and one immediately following the second game. When the Browns left for Baltimore in 1954, the station reached an agreement with St. Louis's remaining baseball team, the Cardinals, to televise all 77 of their road games. To add to the fan base's sports fix, the station also aired roller derby, which was very popular at the time.

COURTESY OF ST. LOUIS
MEDIA HISTORY FOUNDATION

sport back in his hometown. But he was also concerned that if local wrestling was televised, people would sit at home and watch for free rather than paying for tickets to the live events. Without a paying gate, how could he cover costs? Over the course of the 1950s, that mindset would change. Sam looked for ways to make fans at home envious of those attending so that they would want to be ringside. But KPLR-TV would not be the first St. Louis television station to air locally produced and promoted wrestling matches in Sam's hometown.

MAT MOMENTS

IN A JULY 1956 ARTICLE in *Boxing and Wrestling* magazine titled "Will TV Ruin Wrestling?," Sam Muchnick wrote, "One of the most heated controversies in the sports world today is whether Television helps or hurts attendances at sporting events. The people in wrestling have a ready answer. Live television of wrestling shows, that is an actual T.V. cast of a wrestling card, staged in an auditorium before a large audience, has in most cases been beneficial because it has put the sport into millions of homes, and as a result many new fans have been created who perhaps never had sat in on the bouts before." Considering baseball and boxing had become big television draws in these early years of television, it is interesting to note Muchnick's surprising statement, which may indicate that his thinking had turned toward televised live wrestling. He continued, "Commercial sponsors will inform you that live televised wrestling has greater viewing audiences, and sells their products more than any of the other sports events seen on the video screen."

In 1953, while St. Louisans continued to watch wrestling from Chicago, Muchnick began working on a proposal with KSD-TV to determine what it would take to televise local matches. His due diligence included creating plans for a venue and support staff, as well as paying wrestlers, promoters, and all associated television expenses. He even created SAMAR Television Wrestling as a "Cooperative of the Sam Muchnick Sports Attractions and the Mississippi Valley Sports Club." To ensure the venture remained profitable, Muchnick even got a sponsor for his program, Stag Beer. Sam's wrestling show hit the local airwaves on Saturday evening, May 9, 1953, from 9:30 to 11 o'clock. It was repeated on Tuesday nights from 11:30 p.m. to 12:30 a.m. The new show, titled *Wrestling from the St. Louis House*, would replace the matches the station had previously been showing from the Marigold. In one of local television's early programming battles, WTVI then quickly added the Chicago promotion to their schedule.

COURTESY OF JIM ANDERSON

COURTESY OF CODY KNIPPING

SATURDAY NIGHT'S
(October 16, 1954)

Program

MAIN EVENT

"WILD" BILL
LONGSON vs. **LU KIM**

(245) St. Louis, Mo.   (280) Manchuria

FIRST EVENT

DUTCH   JOE
HEFNER vs. **MILLICH**

(245) Sherman, Tex.   (229) St. Louis, Mo.

SECOND EVENT

MIKE   DAVE
PAIDOUSIS vs. **JONS**

(238) Steubenville, O.   (226) London, Eng.

THIRD EVENT

CARLOS   BOB
RODRIGUEZ vs. **LEIPLER**

(225) St. Louis, Mo.   (232) Buffalo, N. Y.

FOURTH EVENT

FRANK   JOE
ALTMAN vs. **TANGARO**

(239) Kansas City   (232) Salt Lake City

FINAL EVENT

BILL   RAY
McDANIEL vs. **ECKERT**

(235) St. Louis, Mo.   (250) California, Mo.

Time of first match—8:45 P. M. Tickets go on sale at St. Louis House at 5:30 P. M. Advance ticket sale tomorrow (Saturday) from 9:15 A. M. to 4 P. M. at Mezzanine 8, Arcade Bldg. No telephone reservations. For information, call GEneva 6-4400 or CHestnut 1-2273.

Wrestling's Greatest Stars Appear Every Saturday Night On St. Louis House Programs

Wrestling's greatest stars will be seen every Saturday night on the programs at St. Louis House, 2345 Lafayette Ave.

Promoter Sam Muchnick and the Mississippi Valley Sports Club have combined their wrestling enterprises under the name of "Samar Wrestling" in order to procure the tops in the mat sport for these Saturday night programs.

Besides the world's heavyweight champion, Lou Thesz, a number of outstanding mat stars appear regularly on the Saturday night cards. Included are: Buddy Rogers, Killer Kowalski, Pat O'Connor, Joe Tangaro, Guy Brunetti, "Wild" Bill Longson, Ray Eckert, Don Leo Jonathan, Cyclone Anaya, Lu Kim, and many others.

The reserved seat sale for these Saturday night cards gets under way each Thursday morning at 9:15 at Mezzanine 8, Arcade Bldg., and in the lobby of Hotel Claridge, 18th and Locust. (The Claridge box office is closed on Saturday). The St. Louis House box office opens at 5:30 p. m. on Saturday.

Because of the limited seating capacity of St. Louis House, tickets are sold on a first-come, first-served basis. For that reason, fans are urged to buy their tickets early.

For the convenience of persons attending the matches, tickets are sold at St. Louis House for the following Saturday night's program.

Ticket prices are: $1, $2 and $3.

World's Greatest Wrestling!
Saturday 9:30 p.m. KSD-TV
Wild Bill Longson v s. **The Great Zorra**
Former heavyweight champion   Famous French strongman and Olympic star

PLUS A STRONG SUPPORTING CARD OF TV FAVORITES

Televised From St. Louis House

● Starting Saturday night, St. Louis makes its bow as wrestling capital of the world with the new Stag Beer series of Saturday night matches of championship caliber. The bouts will originate at St. Louis House Auditorium, 2345 Lafayette. Preliminaries will start at 8:45 p.m. The telecast will begin at 9:30 p.m.

Big Celebrity Show During Intermission

● Some of the leading public and sports figures of the Greater St. Louis Area will make their appearance during the Stag wrestling intermission show at about 10 o'clock. World Champion Lou Thesz, the all-time wrestling great, Strangler Lewis, Sam Muchnick, St. Louis wrestling promoter and president of the National Wrestling Alliance will be interviewed.

Sponsored by  **Stag** BEER

The Beer That Tastes Better Because It's SUGAR-FREE As Beer Can Be!

The Griesedieck Western Brewery Company

Belleville, Illinois   St. Louis, Missouri

Program sheet from the St. Louis House—very reasonable ticket prices

WRESTLING -- St. Louis House
(2345 Lafayette Ave.—at Jefferson)
NEXT FRIDAY, DEC. 13—8:30 P. M.
Main Event—4-Man Tag Team Match—
JACKIE & DON FARGO vs. **BOBBY BRUNS & RAY STEVENS**
GIRLS' BOUT—MARY JANE MULL vs. JO ANN MULLENNIE
ALSO: TOM BRADLEY vs. "TEX" RILEY;
BARNEY (THE CHEST) BERNARD vs. KEN KENNETH.
Admission—$1, $2, $2.50
On Sale: Mez. 8, Arcade Bldg., and Stix, Baer & Fuller (Westroads).
Also—After 5:30 p.m. Dec. 13 at St. Louis House.

WRESTLING
From the St. Louis House
TONIGHT
and Every Saturday Night at 9:30 p.m. over
KSD-TV
100,000 Watts On Channel 5

Gagne and Thesz
in the ring

A May 3, 1953, TV Preview in the *St. Louis Post-Dispatch* a week before *Wrestling from the St. Louis House*'s premiere reported that, according to Sam Muchnick, "the opening telecast will feature two real wrestling stars and that he is signing Lou Thesz, Verne Gagne and other wrestlers of note from the East and the Pacific Coasts for matches in the St. Louis House. It is expected that there will be interviews and quizzes in the wrestling telecast intermission." Throughout the show's history, the matches were held at the St. Louis House at 2345 Lafayette Avenue, located just east of that street's intersection with Jefferson Avenue. It would air every week (104 shows) until April 30, 1955, when the program lost the necessary sponsorship and was halted due to lack of financial support. Local televised wrestling matches then went dark for the next four years. During this period, featured professional wrestling events continued at the Arena and Kiel Auditorium, with title matches, tag teams, and even women brawlers, but these were not the studio matches that would soon become the foundation of local wrestling from the studio of KPLR-TV.

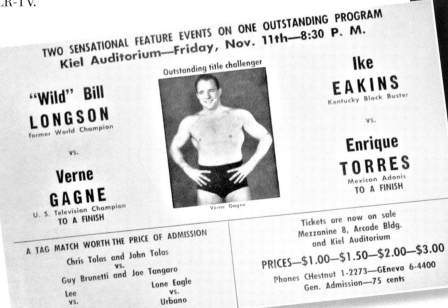

TWO SENSATIONAL FEATURE EVENTS ON ONE OUTSTANDING PROGRAM
Kiel Auditorium—Friday, Nov. 11th—8:30 P. M.

Outstanding title challenger

"Wild" Bill LONGSON
former World Champion

vs.

Verne GAGNE
U. S. Television Champion
TO A FINISH

Verne Gagne

Ike EAKINS
Kentucky Block Buster

vs.

Enrique TORRES
Mexican Adonis
TO A FINISH

A TAG MATCH WORTH THE PRICE OF ADMISSION
Chris Tolas and John Tolas
vs.
Guy Brunetti and Joe Tangaro

Lee
vs.
Hutton

Lone Eagle
vs.
Urbano

Tickets are now on sale
Mezzanine 8, Arcade Bldg.
and Kiel Auditorium

PRICES—$1.00—$1.50—$2.00—$3.00
Phones CHestnut 1-2273—GEneva 6-4400
Gen. Admission—75 cents

KSD-TV cameraman capturing the action
COURTESY OF ST. LOUIS MEDIA HISTORY
FOUNDATION

THE STAGE IS SET WITHIN THE CHASE

IF THE *WRESTLING AT THE CHASE* television program that lasted from 1959 to 1983 is considered the happy marriage of wrestling and television, then a conversation between Sam Muchnick and Harold Koplar that took place on an airplane in 1958 led to the engagement. The question-turned-proposal was about how professional wrestling could once again be brought into living rooms across the St. Louis region in order to expand the sport's fan base to hundreds of thousands of fans. Muchnick had the product, and Koplar had the setting—with the Chase Park Plaza Hotel—and also the means when St. Louis's newest television station hit the airwaves.

Harold Koplar, affectionately known as "HK," followed his father Sam's steps in owning and operating the Chase Park Plaza Hotel. In late April 1959, he also launched a new independent television station in St. Louis as an entertainment extension of his hotel enterprise. As noted in Koplar's

Sam Koplar (*left*) and his son Harold, a.k.a. "HK"
COURTESY OF SAM KOPLAR

Ted Koplar
COURTESY OF BOB AND
SAM KOPLAR

QUALITY DAIRY IS SPONSORING KHOURY LEAGUE BASEBALL on KPLR-TV Channel 11 THIS YEAR

FACTS YOU SHOULD KNOW ABOUT THE KHOURY LEAGUE

Khoury League was the first to have an "All-Star Game" in a major league baseball park for players in all age brackets (Busch Stadium here in St. Louis).

ALWAYS SCORE WITH KING QUALITY PRODUCTS "NONE BETTER"

QUALITY DAIRY CO.
ST. LOUIS, MO.
EV. 1-6000

FACTS YOU SHOULD KNOW ABOUT THE KHOURY LEAGUE

Khoury League was the first organization to provide post-season play-offs for all teams with others of equal standing in other leagues.

ALWAYS SCORE WITH KING QUALITY PRODUCTS "NONE BETTER"

QUALITY DAIRY CO.
ST. LOUIS, MO.
EV. 1-6000

COURTESY OF THE AUTHOR

publications, KPLR-TV was one of the nation's first independent VHF (very high frequency) stations, and through HK's and his son Ted's leadership it would soon be recognized as the number-one independent station in the country. Initially the television operations were located inside the Chase Park Plaza Hotel with the call sign KPLR-TV (the call letters came from a vowel-less version of the Koplar name). Later the station would move to a building with an expanded studio adjacent to his hotel. With his startup independent television network, Koplar was always looking for additional programming and viewership to cover his revenue needs. There was even a time during this period that the initial lack of programming resulted in the station showing Khoury League youth baseball games to cover the airtime. In the meantime, KPLR-TV began mixing movies into their programming along with the very successful St. Louis Hawks National Basketball Association games. The Hawks were NBA champions in 1958 and runners-up in 1957, 1960, and 1961. The station also established local programming that soon took on cult status, including shows like *Captain 11's Showboat* and *Space Patrol*. With former *Ziegfeld Follies* vaudeville actor Harry Fender as the Captain, the *Showboat* was an after-school kids program featuring *Three Stooges* shorts with school-age kids in studio for a ride on the Captain's Showboat. *Wrestling at the Chase* would soon add to the magic of the station. The engagement with Muchnick's wrestling conglomerate became the marriage that put KPLR-TV on the national map.

In addition to now having the television pipeline that would bring wrestling into everyone's

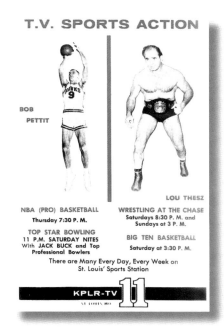

T.V. SPORTS ACTION

BOB PETTIT

LOU THESZ

NBA (PRO) BASKETBALL
Thursday 7:30 P. M.

WRESTLING AT THE CHASE
Saturdays 8:30 P. M. and Sundays at 3 P. M.

TOP STAR BOWLING
11 P.M. SATURDAY NITES
With JACK BUCK and Top Professional Bowlers

BIG TEN BASKETBALL
Saturday at 3:30 P. M.

There are Many Every Day, Every Week on St. Louis' Sports Station

KPLR-TV 11
ST. LOUIS MO

COURTESY OF ST. LOUIS MEDIA HISTORY FOUNDATION

COURTESY OF ST. LOUIS MEDIA HISTORY FOUNDATION

The Three Stooges visit *Captain 11's Showboat.*

COURTESY OF ST. LOUIS MEDIA HISTORY FOUNDATION

MAT MOMENTS

IT'S LIKELY INCONCEIVABLE THAT TODAY'S youth could comprehend a world in which a television set had only three, four, or perhaps five working channels and that television programming was not offered 24 hours a day, generally going off the air between midnight and 5:00 a.m. During this period, television sets were a sizable piece of furniture, usually in the living room. The set consisted of a very large wooden cabinet filled with many tubes that projected onto a very small picture screen in front. The screen's picture was often a grainy shade of gray that had to be regularly adjusted by the movement of a pair of rabbit-ears antenna on the top of the set in order to have a relatively clear and focused picture. Television viewers oftentimes placed aluminum foil between the rabbit ears to try and improve the clarity of the picture. Such was the setting for the premiere of Koplar's station on the St. Louis airwaves on April 28, 1959. St. Louis at that time had only three primary national network affiliate channels (ABC, CBS, and NBC) and a channel representing the Public Broadcasting Service (PBS). KPLR-TV would be the city's fifth. Inside the Chase's Khorassan Room, the matches were covered by three cameras. Former KPLR-TV engineer Wayne Anderson noted that there was one camera in a balcony area for the main ring coverage and two other cameras on the floor. During these early days of television, handheld video cameras had not yet been invented.

COURTESY OF GARY BRANDENBURGER

COURTESY OF RANDY LIEBLER

The vast Khorassan Room
and its glittering chandeliers
COURTESY OF THE AUTHOR

The Khorassan Room
decorated for a
society event
COURTESY OF SAM KOPLAR

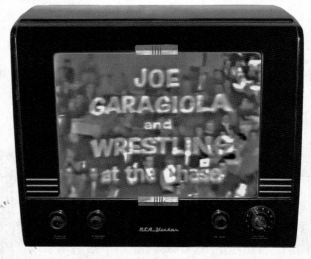

The Khorassan Room hosting a high society event
COURTESY OF MISSOURI HISTORICAL SOCIETY

Wrestling under the chic chandeliers of the Chase Park Plaza's Khorassan Room

home, Harold Koplar also had the city's premier venue to enhance wrestling's image and social standing—the grand ballroom of his very own hotel. For decades the Chase continued to be the place to be and the place to be seen by well-to-do travelers and St. Louisans as well. Beginning in May 1959, it also became a very special place in the hearts of less fancy St. Louisans. The hotel's fabled Khorassan Room historically had been reserved for the city's most prestigious events. The heralded Veiled Prophet and Muny Opera organizations were among those that hosted their black-tie extravaganzas in the spacious and elegant Khorassan Room. While those events continued, the Khorassan Room also took center stage each week in the televised world of professional wrestling by hosting the *Wrestling at the Chase* program. The show became an open invitation to hundreds of thousands of St. Louisans to enter the glamorous Chase for a weekly visit, albeit on television.

Opening credits to early
Wrestling at the Chase

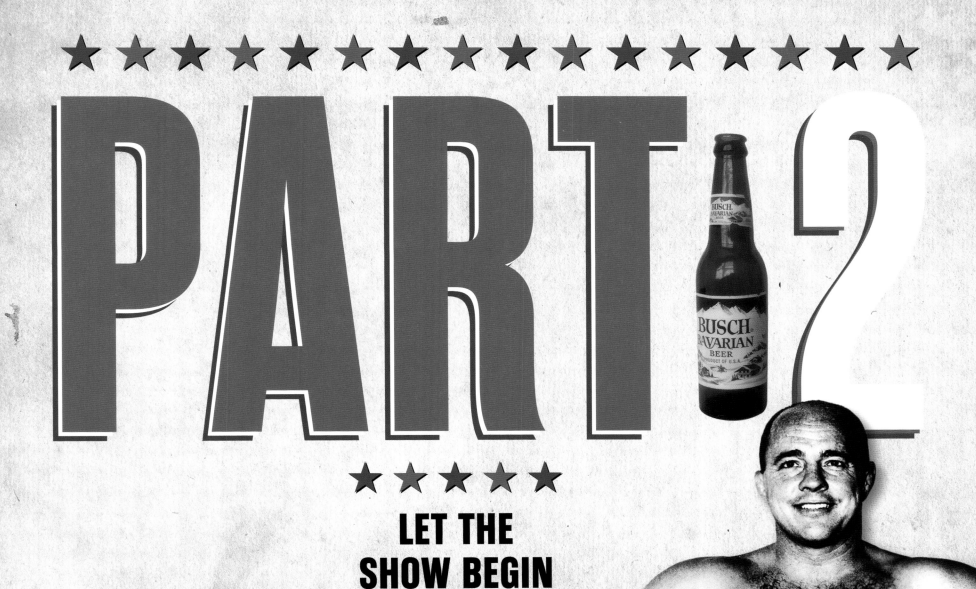

PART 2

LET THE SHOW BEGIN

The two men who turned an airplane flight into the ride of a lifetime

PROMOTER
SAM MUCHNICK

KPLR OWNER
HAROLD KOPLAR

Verne Gagne, 1964
COURTESY OF WIKIMEDIA
COMMMONS

BEER BOTTLE COURTESY OF
JIM ANDERSON

THE BELL RINGS FOR WRESTLING AT THE CHASE

EVERYONE WAS READY for *Wrestling at the Chase*'s television premiere on Saturday, May 23, 1959. Billboards across the city heralded the program high and low while taxicabs hawked the program throughout rush hour traffic. The clang of the ringside bell launched the program that would become one of the longest-running independent programs in St. Louis television history when it ended its run on September 10, 1983. It would become one of the highest-rated programs as well. At times the show had an audience of over 100,000 viewers. Only the local news or locally produced St. Louis Cardinals baseball games drew more viewers in the early days of television programming. Approximately 1,100 shows were broadcast during the program's 24-year run. And nearly every child and adult of that generation who lived in St. Louis during those years has a memory of the program.

PHOTOS COURTESY OF ST. LOUIS
MEDIA HISTORY FOUNDATION

The premise of the show was explained in a letter from Sam Muchnick to Lou Thesz. In the days leading up to *Wrestling at the Chase*'s premiere, newspaper advertisements showcased KPLR-TV's program as "Joe Garagiola and Wrestling at the Chase, 9 to 10 P.M. Every Saturday Night."

Original *Wrestling at the Chase* film presented to Joe Garagiola
COURTESY OF RANDY LIEBLER

May 8, 1959

Mr. Lou Thesz
8231 Camino Del Oro
LaJolla, California

Dear Lou:

It looks like we are about to close a deal for a television show. This would be something unique, as it would be in the Khorssan Room of the Chase Hotel. The matches would be taped for Saturday night shows. The sponsor wants the shows on Saturdays, but with the Khorssan Room unavailable on Saturdays, they will, for the time being, have to be taped on Mondays.

The deal has not been closed, as yet, as there are several things to be worked out. Especially what will be done with the tapes after their first showings. You know, if we don't have control of these tapes, they can develop into monsters, and that's why you have to be careful.

Incidentally, have you been receiving any money from the Chicago films? The reason I ask, is because they recently showed your match with Rogers, in Chicago, on film in Kansas City. That match was really a long time ago.

If we work this out, would you like to come in for a week at a time here, working St. Louis TV and filling out the rest of the week? After two or three appearances, we would be ready for some big shows in the Auditorium.

Incidentally, Joe Garagiola is scheduled to be the announcer of this show, if everything works out okay.

Jeff. Helen and I, and the kids send our love to you, Fredda and

Sincerely,

Sam Muchnick

SMmn

Muchnick's premise for the show is explained to Lou Thesz a little more than a month before the show's premiere.
COURTESY OF RANDY LIEBLER

Gorgeous George Wagner (*left*) taunts his opponent.
COURTESY OF GETTY IMAGES

The first advertisement noted that the show would feature "such great wrestlers as Gorgeous George, the Mighty Atlas, Whipper Billy Watson, [and] Rip Hawk." The wrestling card for that first night was actually Jim LaRock vs. the Mighty Atlas, Rip Hawk vs. Ray Spindola, and Whipper Billy Watson vs. Bob Orton. Garagiola would provide commentary during the evening's matches, and the local sports hero's mere presence added to the legitimacy and standing of the program.

Bob Orton

Whipper Billy Watson

Rip Hawk

The Mighty Atlas

MAT MOMENTS

UNBEKNOWNST TO MOST, while *Wrestling at the Chase* soon became Saturday night "must-see TV" for mid-America, it wasn't live television. Although the show aired on Saturday evenings, it was initially taped on Monday evening and then broadcast the following weekend. It was also re-aired on Sundays at different times, and there was a period when it was shown on Wednesday nights as well. Throughout its run, *Wrestling at the Chase* was filmed on different days and different times for its weekend airings. That way, the Khorassan Room could be used each weekend for the lavish balls and dinners of St. Louis's social seasons. But it really didn't matter which night it was taped as long as the bell rang on Saturday nights for the thousands of fans sitting on the edge of their seats in front of their television sets watching legendary grapplers matched in the mayhem of their sport.

Fans watching ringside in the Khorassan Room

Joe Garagiola ringside

Joe Garagiola was a native St. Louisan who was beginning his rise to national fame. He had grown up a short distance from the Chase Hotel in St. Louis's storied Italian immigrant community known as "The Hill." He and his neighbor and close friend from across the street, Yogi Berra, had both made it to the major leagues as catchers. Yogi's Hall of Fame career began with the New York Yankees, while Joe's began with his hometown Cardinals. Joe's nine-year major league career with four different ball clubs ended in 1954, and he signed on as an announcer for Cardinals baseball alongside future Hall of Fame broadcasters Jack Buck and Harry Caray. That eight-year stint, from 1955 to 1962, calling games for the local ball club led him into the national spotlight. Joe began appearing on NBC's *Today* show as well as in baseball broadcast booths around the country as an announcer on NBC's *Game of the Week*. But on that spring night in 1959, it all came together. Koplar with his hotel and television network, Muchnick with his wrestlers, and hometown boy Joe Garagiola stepping into the ring and commentator's chair hosting the very first episode of *Wrestling at the Chase.*

Adding to the television backdrop were the fans who filled the Chase Hotel's swank Khorassan Room. It definitely was not a blue-collar crowd filling a dimly lit, smoke-filled wrestling hall, and *Wrestling at the Chase* was definitely not a circus in a gilded palace. In

1999, KPLR-TV did a "Look Back" documentary on the program that included interviews with many of those involved with the program. Former world champion Lou Thesz, a veteran of many tank-town matches in half-lit and battered rings across the country, repeatedly remarked what a pleasure it was to wrestle under the chandeliered lighting and elegance of the Khorassan Room with men in black ties and ladies in evening gowns. Harley Race took it a step further, saying that "going in at that point and time to a world-class hotel, walking into a room that seated probably eight to nine hundred people, all dressed in evening attire, sitting there, sipping champagne. If that doesn't take you back to the Roman gladiator days. How many people can say they were there and did that."

Ringside fans dressed to the nines

Even hometown hero Joe Garagiola echoed the adage that the Chase Hotel was still the place to be in 1959 as *Wrestling at the Chase* unfolded. As a youth, the hotel was always something special to him and his friends and family. "Stop to think about it," he said. "The Chase Hotel. When I was growing up, we used to drive by and wish that we would win a contest or have enough money to go inside the Chase Hotel . . . and now they're going to have wrestling in the Khorassan Room . . . and the Khorassan Room was the most beautiful room probably in the state or this area . . . and this is where they were going to have wrestling. And I thought, what a concept. This is so different. I mean wrestling and the Khorassan Room. But I tell you, it turned out to be an event. People would clamor to come here. It got to be the place to be." Joe soon began describing the audience during the telecast as being filled with "closet fans." These fans described were people of prominence like doctors, lawyers, and politicians sitting ringside weekly just to be seen. Joe's brother Mickey probably summarized the setting best with the simple quip, "Wrestling now has class!" For so many others, like lifelong wrestling fan Jerry Bullion, watching *Wrestling at the Chase* was a true family affair as he and his fifteen family members gathered around the old black-and-white television set cheering on the action just like they were ringside in the Khorassan Room of the Chase Hotel.

The audience was seated around a wrestling ring set up in the middle of the large, glamorous ballroom that could handle a capacity crowd of up to 1,000 patrons. The tickets to the event were free, and the general public could obtain them simply by sending a self-addressed envelope to the KPLR-TV studio. There, the requests would be put on a long waiting list. Just like the popular live television show of today's generation, *Saturday Night Live*, *Wrestling at the Chase*'s popularity meant that demand for tickets regularly resulted in a waiting list of three to four months.

MAT MOMENTS

WHILE THE AUDIENCE AND THE RING WERE POSITIONED in such a regal setting, legendary *Globe-Democrat* sportswriter Bob Burnes noted in a 1959 column that the wrestlers and referees had a little different setup. The emphasis being on little. "The televised wrestling in the Khorassan Room at the Chase is proving quite a success . . . and everybody seems to be enjoying it. The whole thing is staged on an elaborate scale with one exception. . . . All of the wrestlers and referees are herded into one small room at the southeast end of the building before and after their appearances in the ring. This includes men who have been mauling and whacking at each other or are about to do so. . . . Just on general principles for a variety of reasons, somebody should figure out some way to keep opponents separated . . . and the referees as far as possible away from them."

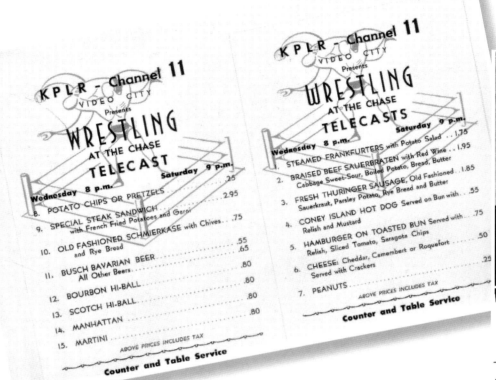

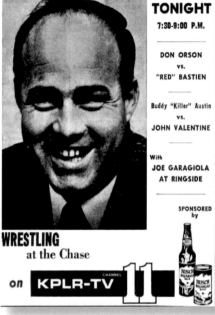

TONIGHT
7:30-9:00 P.M.

DON ORSON
vs.
"RED" BASTIEN

Buddy "Killer" Austin
vs.
JOHN VALENTINE

With
JOE GARAGIOLA
AT RINGSIDE

SPONSORED
by

WRESTLING
at the Chase
on KPLR-TV 11

COURTESY OF ST.
LOUIS MEDIA HISTORY
FOUNDATION

COURTESY OF
JIM ANDERSON

With tickets in hand and seated ringside, fans had to pay for their food and drink. Advertising promoted Chase staff serving tasty Bavarian-style food consisting of pitchers of beer and brats to add to the atmosphere. After all, Busch Bavarian Beer was the program's sponsor. What a sight it must have been to see those closet fans that Joe Garagiola described dressed to the nines drinking their beer and eating brats ringside at tables donned with red and white checkered tablecloths. There are many tales of men telling their sweethearts to get dressed up because they had tickets to the Chase, only for the ladies to discover later that they wouldn't be seeing an entertainer like Frank Sinatra, Rosemary Clooney, or Tony Martin in the Chase Club or Starlight Room but would instead be sitting ringside in the hotel's Khorassan Room. But in the end it didn't seem to matter, because the Chase was the place to be, and they were there and part of the hottest show in mid-America.

Fans seated ringside around tables with checkered tablecloths

MAT
MOMENTS

WHILE THE STYLISHLY DRESSED WOMEN in the audience may have initially been miffed to find that they weren't sitting center stage listening and humming to the golden voice of Frank Sinatra, to television viewers the loudest screams and carrying-on during matches seemed to come from the ladies. Jimmy Powers's Powerhouse column in the *St. Louis Globe-Democrat* on July 5, 1959, succinctly summed up the situation when he quoted a famous wrestling referee from the program: "I am beginning to give up on women. I just can't understand them. My experience as a wrestling referee convinces me women are definitely more blood-thirsty than men. They are the ones who howl loudest for that gory stuff." All a person has to do is watch the old tapes of matches from *Wrestling at the Chase* to see how hostile and loud the female fans were.

Women heckling the Baron during the program's match

But it wasn't just the women ringside who howled it up. It was done at home as well. Restaurateur Emil Pozzo and his family love to talk about his grandmother Guilina going to her bedroom and shutting the door. She wanted to watch *Wrestling at the Chase* without anyone disturbing her. Behind the closed door, they could hear her screaming at the wrestlers and referees throughout the program. Once in a while, Emil looked in on her, and she would be out of her chair, on her knees counting the grappler out in unison with the referee.

Even as far back as March 1950, the *St. Louis Post-Dispatch* highlighted a headline story: "Ladies Love Wrestling! . . . Even Grandmas Go for Grunters." The article notes that "for some time it has been apparent that to a great many American women the sight of a heavyweight wrestler hurtling through the dank night air is a thing of beauty to behold." The article continues, "The number of women at grunt-and-groan shows has soared astronomically in the last five years. The odd result is that wrestlers now rival crooners, movie actors, and football stars in the affections of a considerable group of bobby-soxers, young matrons, middle-aged hausfraus and grandmothers alike." And *Wrestling at the Chase* was bringing that fascination right into these women's very own homes each week. The show was well received right off the bat. The *St. Louis Globe-Democrat*'s TV-radio editor, Pete Rahn, noted on June 1, 1959, "Wrestling fans and St. Louis promoter Sam Muchnick are undoubtedly very happy that Channel 11 has made room in its schedules for their favorite sport. Wrestling from the Chase Hotel! No less. And from the fabled Khorassan Room of the Chase at that. Lands sakes! I always thought those gilded and carpeted precincts were reserved for such special occasions as the Veiled Prophet's doin's and the Muny Opera's black-tie Guarantor's Ball. But here's Big Chief somebody or the other (complete with Apache haircut and headdress) belting the bejabbers out of his opponents, while the hamburger-chomping, beer-guzzling crowd makes with the war whoops."

Ladies Love Wrestling!

Gripped by excitement of their favorite sport, a row of lady wrestling fans happily await triumph of their hero.

Even grandmas go for the grunters

By FRANK De BLOIS

FOR SOME TIME NOW it has been apparent that to a great many American women the sight of a heavyweight wrestler hurtling through the dank night air is a thing of beauty to behold.

Although sociologists and psychiatrists haven't quite figured out the reason for this strange phenomenon, it is now a recognized fact that the number of women at grunt-and-groan shows has soared astronomically during the past five years. The odd result is that wrestlers now rival crooners, movie actors and football stars in the affections of a considerable group of bobby-soxers, young matrons, middle-aged *hausfraus* and grandmothers alike.

Bad Night for the Ape Man

Within the past year, feminine fans have showered their favorite wrestlers with tons of candy, flowers, clothing and proposals of marriage. They have attacked wrestlers, whose tactics they disapproved, with nails, teeth, shoes, hairpins—and on one unhappy occasion a rusty hatchet.

Through painful experience, wrestlers have developed a keen analysis of this peculiar behaviour problem. "It's simple," a current mat favorite remarked recently. "Women like to look at my muscles the same way as I like to look at Betty Grable's legs."

But in the opinion of the Ape Man, a prominent contemporary wrestler who is taken to and from his work every night in a cage, women like wrestling because, unlike almost any other form of spectator activity, it gives them an opportunity to release suppressed emotions.

"They can't yell and scream at home," said the Ape Man, "but they certainly seem to feel free to raise cain at a wrestling show."

The Ape Man knows whereof he speaks. In Rochester, N. Y., last summer a lady climbed through the ropes while he was throttling an opponent and stroked him on the head with a Pepsi-Cola bottle. He finally restrained her with a half-nelson.

This experience was duplicated some months later in La Grange, Ga., when a wrestler named Count Dracula was interrupted in the act of breaking another wrestler's toe by a lady who leaped into the ring wielding a rusty hatchet. The Count left the hall under police escort.

Some of wrestling's most erudite students are stumped by the performance of its leading feminine followers. Guy Lebow, whose television accounts of grunting bouts in New York have thousands of regular listeners, has been studying his audiences for years but claims that today he remains as mystified as ever.

"On occasions," Lebow says somewhat wistfully, "the lady wrestling fan seems to lose contact with reality. The other day a lady telephoned me

GORGEOUS GEORGE (in air) is idol of feminine fans from Sag Harbor to Seattle.

to complain that her teen-age daughter, an admirer of a heavyweight named Chief Little Wolf, had shaved her hair off Apache-style in imitation of her hero."

TV, Lebow believes, has brought one big hazard to wrestlers: girls.

"On TV," the announcer says, "the girls get to recognize their favorites and when they see them in public they often swoon. This can become very wearing on a man."

Hatpins, Too; Even Oaths

During a recent wrestling match in Brooklyn, the intensity of feminine emotion reached a state seldom seen since the funeral of Rudolph Valentino. The subject of the fans' ardor on this occasion was the Golden Superman, a large mass of fatty tissue billed as "the world's most perfectly proportioned mortal." The object of the fans rage was the Bat, whose technique consists of flapping his arms up and down and springing at his opponent's throat.

When he entered the ring Superman was greeted with sighs, moans, whoops of joy and semi-hysterical laughter. His opponent was treated to a chorus of curses and mutterings.

As the bout progressed, a lady in the third row heaved a tainted mackerel into the ring and a fan named Hat Pin Mary reached through the ropes and jabbed the Bat with a three-inch poinard.

When they left the ring Superman was showered with flowers and the Bat was sprinkled with oaths.

"It was nothing," the latter said while relaxing in his shower ten minutes later. "Why, in Buffalo last week a lady jumped into the ring, hit me over the eye with her shoe, pulled out a fistful of my hair and jumped up and down on my instep. Those ladies in Buffalo are full of enthusiasm!"

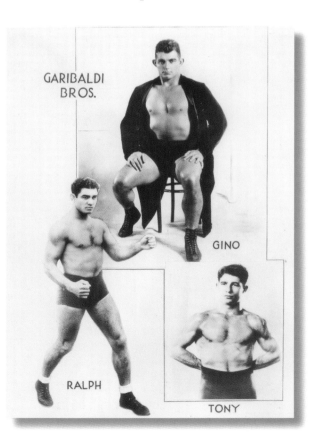

GARIBALDI BROS.

GINO

RALPH

TONY

St. Louis's Garibaldi Brothers

COURTESY OF KARA VANINGER

COURTESY OF NEWSPAPERS.COM

Bobo Brazil flips champion Buddy Austin on his head guard.

51

THEY MADE YOU BELIEVE

WHILE THE FOCUS of televised wrestling was truly the action in the ring, the translation of that action by the program's television commentators made it even more magical and real for the thousands of fans watching at home. Although he never attended a taping of *Wrestling at the Chase*, Hall of Fame sportscaster Bob Costas was a tangent fan at times. He was never involved with the program but would occasionally watch it on television once he came to St. Louis in 1974 and often found himself addressing questions and comments on KMOX radio's *Sports Open Line* call-in show that he hosted. Bob had grown up in New York and was a fan of an independent television station that also aired *The Three Stooges* and *Superman* programs as well as professional wrestling. His experiences were the same as those of so many youngsters in his new hometown. What had enamored Bob as he watched professional wrestling back home in New York were the announcers and how they made this pseudo-sport seem so real. Bob noted that:

> "Despite the frequent absurdity of the wrestler's antics in the ring, announcers like "Mean" Gene Okerlund treated the action with dead seriousness. Here were these announcers dressed in tuxedos adding to the atmosphere of the event with their observations of every move as though it were a lethal or paralyzing attack that would have fans watching at home on the edge of their seats. These announcers lent excitement with their vocal reactions to grapplers' holds and tosses while adding a touch of serious commentary to make it all seem real and believable."

St. Louis's *Wrestling at the Chase* was no different, and the program came to have some of the best announcers in the business, which added to the program's success and mystique. Fans at home reacted with outbursts of their own, often screaming at the television set trying to guide their favorite wrestler to victory. Joe Garagiola provided the play-by-play commentary for the first four years, until 1962. His brother served as ring announcer. Joe left for New York in 1963, and Don Cunningham became his replacement but unfortunately passed away in December of the following year. A former baseball and basketball announcer in Buffalo, New York, Cunningham had come to St. Louis in 1959 to broadcast games for the St. Louis Hawks that would also be televised on the newly christened KPLR-TV station. He later became KPLR-TV's sports director. However, Cunningham's career hosting *Wrestling at the Chase* was short lived. In August 1963, he was seriously injured when the car he was driving plunged down a 30-foot embankment after he missed a curve on his way home after work.[12] While he was recuperating, George Abel stepped up to the microphone to provide wrestling commentary. In time, Cunningham recovered and was back at ringside and announced matches throughout 1964, until he was found dead at his home that December. He died due to the effects of barbiturates and alcohol.[13]

George Abel

A new host and commentator was needed, and George Abel returned ringside. He was no novice to the wrestling game. Back in 1954, he had been the ringside announcer for KSD-TV's *Wrestling from the St. Louis House* program. By 1964, Abel had already become a St. Louis television institution. Growing up in St. Louis and attending both McBride High School and Saint Louis University, he had begun his hometown career on the air in 1943 at KSD Radio before moving over to St. Louis's first television station KSD-TV in 1947 as one of its original on-air employees. Abel had served as a news and sports announcer and commentator before becoming known to kids across the region as Texas Bruce's sidekick Dry Gulch on the after-school *Wranglers Cartoon Club*. He was also familiar to adults as a do-everything personality on the very popular *Charlotte Peters Show*. His St. Louis television persona only got larger when he took the helm of *Wrestling at the Chase* and kept the chair warm until 1972, when he was joined at the ringside table by Larry Matysik as a regular guest commentator. After nearly a decade ringside, Abel was replaced

Abel as Dry Gulch
COURTESY OF ST. LOUIS MEDIA HISTORY FOUNDATION

DRY GULCH
seen on
"WRANGLERS CLUB
with CORKY the CLOWN"
5
KSD-TV

TOMORROW NIGHT
IS A
BIG! BIG! BIG!
SPORTS NIGHT
ON
KPLR-TV

Don't miss any of the top TV entertainment and excitement of this sensational sports lineup:

8:00 P.M. WRESTLING AT THE CHASE
the nation's "mighty men of the mat" meet in the Khorassan Room with DON CUNNINGHAM adding colorful comments at ringside.

9:00 P.M. STRIKE IT LUCKY BOWLING
Howard Dorsey emcees this new and exciting hour-long show while St. Louis bowlers compete for $6,000 in Giant Jackpot Prizes.

10:00 P.M. SATURDAY SPORTS SPECIAL
Don Cunningham's Sports News Final with special guests Jimmy Conzelman and Football Cardinals' Owner Bill Bidwill.

10:15 P.M. BROWNS RAMS PRO FOOTBALL GAME (LIVE)
Cleveland Browns vs. Los Angeles Rams direct from Los Angeles in this *first live* pro football telecast of the season.

CHANNEL **11** KPLR-TV

SEE THE BEST IN SPORTS SATURDAY
ON
KPLR-TV
<u>STILL</u> THE FIRST IN SPORTS IN ST. LOUIS

Abel in one of Charlotte Peters's sketches
COURTESY OF ST. LOUIS MEDIA HISTORY FOUNDATION

by longtime wrestler-turned-commentator Sam Menacker, and Matysik's title became color commentator. By October 1973, Larry's skills had sharpened to the point where it became his program, with ring announcer Mickey Garagiola sliding alongside as his sidekick for the next decade.

At the time he first appeared on the show on February 12, 1972, Larry Matysik was a part-time police officer from across the Mississippi River in Belleville, Illinois. But more importantly, he had been a longtime protégé of Sam Muchnick with more than a decade-long career in St. Louis wrestling. In 1963, when Matysik was 16, Muchnick had taken Larry under his wing and offered him work that would lead him to be a publicist, office manager, and booking agent for Sam's St. Louis Wrestling Club. Looking back, Larry's rise in the industry seemed to almost mirror Sam's career path under Tom Packs.

Larry had grown up in Belleville and was attending Southern Illinois University at Edwardsville while also working and learning the wrestling ropes under Muchnick. Larry had majored in professional writing and minored in journalism, but under Sam he majored in all aspects of the wrestling business. Under his boss's oversight, Larry had access to the complete and long history of St. Louis professional wrestling, neatly stored in file cabinets in Muchnick's office in the Claridge Hotel, located at the corner of Eighteenth and Locust Streets in downtown St. Louis. Larry had many duties in the early days under Muchnick's tutelage.

Larry Matysik and George Abel ringside

Larry and Sam

Mickey alongside Larry ringside

54

Sam Menacker with
Gene Kiniski

Sam put Larry's studies to good use by having him take over the writing and mailing of the four-page pamphlet that was distributed about 10 days before every major match at the Arena or Kiel. In addition, Larry became responsible for writing and disseminating news releases as well as match results to local newspapers. As his responsibilities and knowledge continued to grow, he gained important contacts in the sport, the press, and the city. Larry typed and mailed the weekly lineups for *Wrestling at the Chase* to George Abel and Mickey Garagiola, the start of what would later become long-standing ringside partnerships with the two. He also researched and provided George and Mickey with background information on

George Abel and
Mickey Garagiola

the upcoming wrestlers, their feuds, and other pertinent information on typed 3 × 5 index cards.

So as George Abel was waning away from his ringside duties, Larry spent a short time at the announcers' table with former wrestler Sam Menacker before taking over as host on October 13, 1973. He did not merely become the voice of the wrestling series; he rose to be considered one of the top wrestling announcers in the country. Although Matysik occasionally worked the mic for American Wrestling Association events, *Wrestling at the Chase* was his bread and butter, and he stayed with the show through its conclusion in 1983.

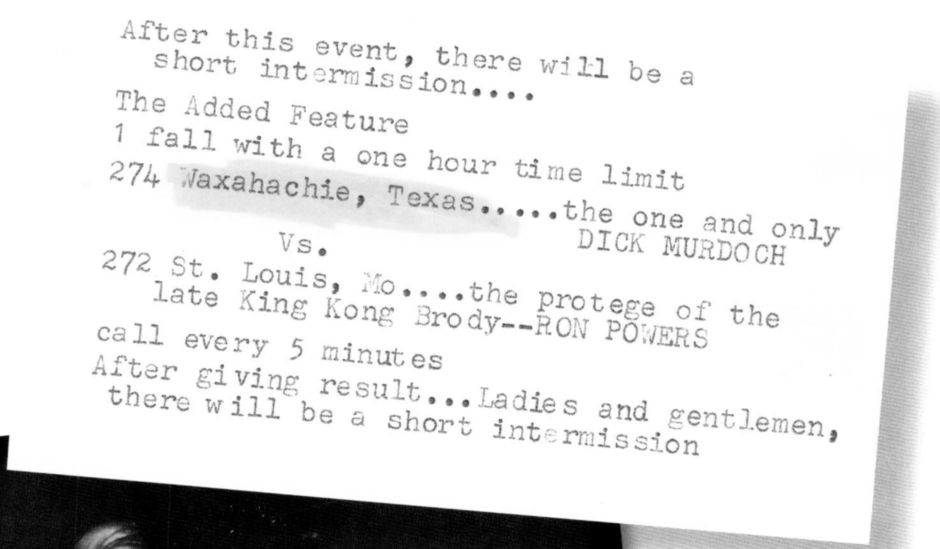

```
After this event, there will be a
     short intermission....
The Added Feature
1 fall with a one hour time limit
274 Waxahachie, Texas.....the one and only
                                  DICK MURDOCH
          Vs.
272 St. Louis, Mo....the protege of the
     late King Kong Brody--RON POWERS
call every 5 minutes
After giving result...Ladies and gentlemen,
     there will be a short intermission
```

COURTESY OF
BOB GARAGIOLA

Referee Charlie Venator
freeing a wrestler tied up
in the ropes

Garagiola (partly hidden),
Matysik, and Menacker
ringside in 1973

COURTESY OF ST. LOUIS MEDIA
HISTORY FOUNDATION

While Garagiola, Cunningham, Abel, and Matysik were the faces of the show and the voices that excited fans at home with their expressive and emotional commentary of each match, there were other key individuals involved with the program. Every match must have a referee inside the ring, and some of the most prominent were Joe Schoenberger, Ed Smith, and Charles Venator. There were also the ring announcers who brought the grapplers together to start each match and would later announce and raise the arm of the winner. Some of the best known were John Curley, Eddie Gromacki, and Joe Garagiola's older brother Mickey. Wrestler Cowboy Bob Orton noted that as the show continued through the years, Mickey Garagiola became known as "the voice of the fan." As the matches were underway, Mickey would sit next to announcer Larry Matysik and occasionally make a comment or two about the match or provide insight on a grappler he would like to see win later on the card.

Brody, Race, and referee Charlie Venator, who worked full-time as a postmaster

The voice of the fan— Mickey Garagiola

COURTESY OF BOB GARAGIOLA

Mickey, Larry, and floor director Ollie Hoffstetter

COURTESY OF MERCANTILE LIBRARY

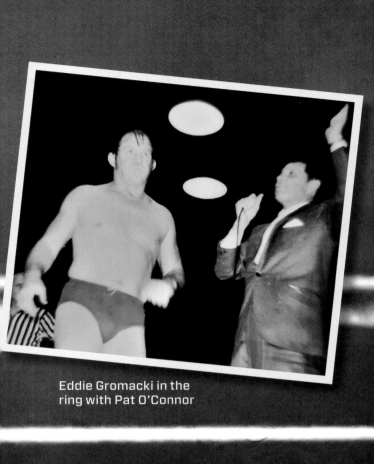
Eddie Gromacki in the
ring with Pat O'Connor

Referee Joe Schoenberger looks
over Lou Thesz and Gene Kiniski.

MAT MOMENTS

THE INCOMPARABLE MICKEY GARAGIOLA. WHILE Mickey became a beloved St. Louis television personality on *Wrestling at the Chase*, he had another moment in the sun, or should I say "bar," that made him a legend in the creation of one of St. Louis's classic culinary treats—toasted ravioli. Mickey had begun his career in 1936 as a busboy and then dishwasher before becoming a waiter for decades at Ruggeri's Restaurant in St. Louis's historic Italian neighborhood known as "The Hill." One night after his shift at Ruggeri's, Mickey and a few other waiters went to another restaurant on the Hill named Oldani's, which was open late. There, a chef named Fritz

had accidently dropped an order of ravioli into hot oil instead of hot water. As the chef sought to rectify his mistake, he sent the deep-fried pasta bits to the bar as an appetizer. Mickey took them, added a little sauce, and voilà, St. Louis's toasted ravioli was born—and with it the legend that Mickey was the first to eat this great St. Louis delicacy. While others say the specialty dish was first created elsewhere, today almost everyone recognizes the tale of Oldani's and of Mickey Garagiola having the first taste. In fact, Mickey backed his claim by firmly stating that he "would bet my house on it."

Do you think Joe Garagiola's business card read, "Mickey's Brother"?

COURTESY OF
BOB GARAGIOLA

Mickey was known to be a shrewd but playful individual. His son Bob provided many insightful stories of Mickey's mischief. For a short period at the start of his work with *Wrestling at the Chase*, Mickey met up with friends on Saturday mornings to hang out and have coffee at a filling-station-turned-auto-repair-shop on the Hill at Bischoff and Marconi Avenues. There, he would find what he called "a pigeon" and make a few bets on that night's wrestling card, which Mickey just happened to have in his pocket. Unbeknownst to the target, the matches had been taped days earlier, and he was setting up his buddies. To avoid letting the cat out of the bag, he would politely throw a few bets, but according to his son Bob, the scam was all in fun until everyone caught on to the taping schedule. It was simply another story of Mickey being Mickey with the boys on the Hill.

Mickey and Bulldog Bob Brown
COURTESY OF BOB GARAGIOLA

Just like his pals, Mickey didn't initially understand that the wrestling matches were fought earlier in the week and that taped matches were televised on Saturday night. When Sam Muchnick initially approached him to be a part of the program with his brother Joe, Mickey turned him down, saying that Saturday night was the biggest night at Ruggeri's Restaurant and he had to work. Sam quickly set the record straight and probably flipped the light bulb in Mickey's head for his hijinks with his pals on the Hill.

One of the fun-loving Mickey's other favorite tricks was played when he would chauffeur the wrestlers to their hotel after the show's filming. While driving, Mickey would spot his prey, usually some youthful driver. He would go into an upset-driver act, honking his horn and flashing his lights in order to get under the other driver's skin. Then, when the two cars came to a stoplight, the drivers would exchange words, which would lead to them stepping out of their cars to settle their beef. As the young man was ready to charge old man Mickey, the hulking likes of Bulldog Bob Brown, Harley Race, or Gene Kiniski would step out of the car behind Mickey. Soon the youth was jumping into his car to get out of there as fast as he could while Mickey and the wrestlers had their laughs. These are just a few of the many stories of the legend of Mickey Garagiola, the ambassador of both *Wrestling at the Chase* and the Hill.

Harley Race and Gene Kiniski

CHANGE IS IN THE AIR

AS THE PROGRAM'S SUCCESS continued from years into decades, there was the need for a change of scenery. After having every match fought and filmed in the Khorassan Room since the program's premiere on that Saturday evening in May 1959, a short move took place after the November 4, 1967, program, although there would be a brief three-month return to the ballroom in 1972. Sharing the always-in-demand Khorassan Room was making scheduling difficult for both the hotel and the television station. The arrangement created other issues that had cost impacts on the producers, promoters, and wrestlers. Many of the wrestlers came to St. Louis not just for the television program but also to fill a wrestling card at

Kiel Auditorium on the previous Friday or Saturday, which forced a layover until Monday's taping at the Chase.

A decision was made to begin filming the program in the KPLR-TV studio, located just on the other side of the back wall of the Khorassan Room stage. No longer would there be the expense of setting up and taking down the television lights, cameras, and other equipment—including the wrestling ring—from the ballroom each week. Prior to the move, the ballroom would have to be refurbished for that week's upcoming galas and then once again reassembled for the wrestling program. It was also around this time that the program began filming in color, which brought additional technical requirements. The new color cameras and cables had become too heavy and too delicate to keep moving. With the relocation to the KPLR-TV studio, wrestlers were no longer grappling under elegant chandeliers in a glamorous ballroom in a ring surrounded by dressed-up fans sitting along rows of tables with checkered tablecloths. The new venue offered a more sterile backdrop with a cozier, downsized audience of about 350 fans. Fans no longer came dressed in formal attire, and the move prompted Larry Matysik to change the program's opening salutation to "From the KPLR studio in the Chase Hotel complex."

The program moved into the KPLR-TV studio to film the matches in color.
COURTESY OF ST. LOUIS MEDIA HISTORY FOUNDATION

The relocation of the ring and fans into the television studio led to one of the biggest changes in the show's history. Taping of matches was no longer an evening date-night experience as it had been for many fans during the last decade and a half. Starting in 1973, three programs were taped on Sundays beginning at 12:30 p.m., which led fans to start lining up outside the KPLR-TV studio on York Avenue all the way around to Lindell Boulevard shortly after 8:00 a.m. Even under the new setup, *Wrestling at the Chase* was still a hot ticket. Changes were needed inside the studio as well. First, the ringside announcing team would need three changes of clothes to host that day's separate programs. The fans in the studio crowd were also impacted. The audience would be rearranged after each program, causing fans to change their seats so that the next show's taping looked like a totally new and fresh audience. Dan Thompson recalls going to the Sunday morning tapings and to accommodate looking like three separate audiences for three weekly shows, "they made everyone in the first 2 rows get up and rotate to the section to our right after each show. [Between takes], we went out in the hallway

and saw all the wrestlers sitting around talking and joking." Despite all these changes, the ringside bell still rang, the combatants still wrestled, and the crowd still loved it. And that is how *Wrestling at the Chase* was filmed for its final decade.

MAT
MOMENTS

WOMEN WOULD ROWDILY SCREAM at the wrestling mayhem inside the ring, but Ted Koplar tells a noteworthy tale about women gathering behind the KPLR-TV studio building. For a long time, he could not figure out why so many women were always standing outside the back of the studio during and after the matches. In time, he realized that along the back of the building there were windows that looked into a balcony upon which these ladies, who over time became known as "ring rats," could see the grapplers walking scantily clad back and forth to the showers. It seems these female fans fancied the wrestlers' moves as much outside the ring as inside!

King Kong Brody

FANS' MEMORIES

WHETHER THEY WATCHED ringside or on television, people's memories of *Wrestling at the Chase* remain vivid today. Here are just a few that might jog your own memory. In looking back at their youth, many adults today remember being forced to go to early church services on Sunday mornings so their parents or grandparents could be back home in time to watch the Sunday replay of their favorite wrestling program. Throughout these stories it seems that the grandparents' love of the program translated into the memories. I

myself remember those Saturday evenings with my grandma making ice cream floats with Dad's root beer and vanilla ice cream before she and I would sit down and watch the program. For others it was a full family experience. Rich Noffke tells a story of how everything (including the house antenna) had to change on Saturday nights so his grandfather could watch *Wrestling at the Chase*. Rich grew up in the farm community of Stewardson, Illinois, about 110 miles northeast of St. Louis. Throughout the week, the family's television antenna attached to the side of the house was aimed north toward the Champaign-Urbana broadcast towers. However, early every Saturday evening his older brothers had the job of reaching out with the pliers to turn the antenna's pole to the south so that grandpa could get a grainy but clear enough picture to watch *Wrestling at the*

PHOTOS COURTESY
OF IRENE MUELLER

Chase. Then on Sunday morning, they had to turn the antenna back to the north for better reception of the regular television programs. Speaking of Sundays and grandparents, Jim Fetsch attended many matches in the Khorassan Room as well as in the KPLR-TV studio, but his most vivid memory of *Wrestling at the Chase* is watching matches at home with his very own "grandma Mac."

"She would sit and curse at the television screen every Sunday morning, telling Baron Von Raschke to 'give him the claw' or hollering at the wrestler on the screen to watch out for a particular move that his opponent had used on him in the last match, which was actually the match she had also watched the night before."

Several fans have relayed stories of a woman with red hair and a beehive hairdo sitting ringside at every show, banging a rubber chicken on the apron of the ring during matches week after week. It turns out her name was Ruth, and she was from across the river in Madison, Illinois. There are just so many special memories from the show, even for those who today don't like to admit they were wrestling fans—shades of Joe Garagiola's "closet fans" comment. In fact, it's really hard to find anyone over the age of 45 who grew up in the St. Louis region and does not have some special, touching memory and moment from *Wrestling at the Chase*.

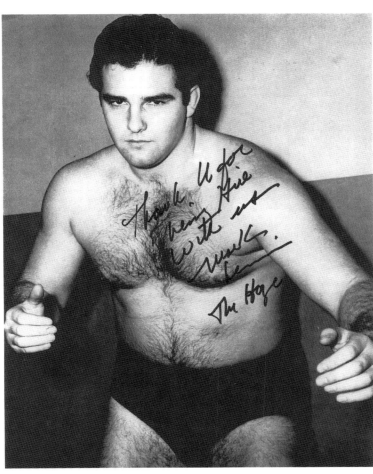

PHOTOS COURTESY
OF IRENE MUELLER

HISTORY REPEATS ITSELF

BY 1982, the pendulum of change would swing once more within the world of professional wrestling in St. Louis. Sam Muchnick had planned on retiring at the end of 1978, but pleas from the fans kept him going. Four years later, after nearly two and a half decades leading the NWA and over forty years in the promotions business, Sam was finally ready to step aside. He sold the St. Louis Wrestling Club to the triumvirate of Verne Gagne, Bob Geigel, and Pat O'Connor. In time, Harley Race would also join that partnership. Also included in that sale was the *Wrestling at the Chase* program. On the night of Friday, January 1, 1982, a sellout crowd of 19,819 packed the Checkerdome (the name of the rebranded Arena during the period that Ralston-Purina owned the building and the St. Louis Blues hockey team) for a farewell salute to Sam Muchnick. It was a wrestling event filled with dignitaries and former wrestlers honoring the man who meant so much to the sport. As so many had said before and since, if there had been no Sam Muchnick, professional wrestling never would have risen to become the phenomenon it became then and is today!

Larry Matysik's position was included in the assets transferred to the trio. As part of the sale of the club, Sam agreed to remain on the ledgers for another year as a consultant, and Larry would remain at the microphone. When Sam's time was up, Matysik, who had spent the last thirteen years in the organization, soon

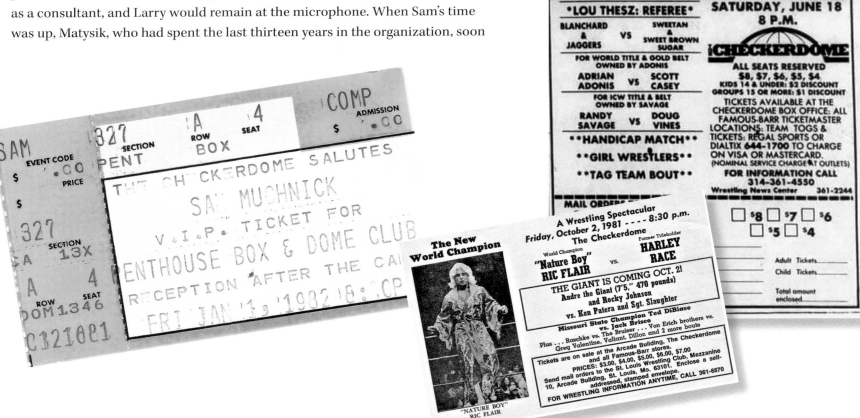

followed. During this time, professional wrestling in St. Louis was being stretched in multiple directions, mainly due to changing philosophies of the sport. No longer associated with his former employers, Matysik began his own promotion company, called St. Louis Wrestling Enterprises, to go head to head with the trio's St. Louis Wrestling Club. Soon playbills were in place from each entity hawking matches to be held in St. Louis. Matysik's matches were held at the Checkerdome, while the St. Louis Wrestling Club continued to use the venerable Kiel Auditorium. Once again, history repeated itself. Matysik was out on his own now, somewhat mirroring his mentor's break from Tom Packs in 1945. Local wrestling fans again

Randy Savage

benefited, with more matches and more talent in town just like they did when Muchnick and Packs played out their feud. While most of the "old guard" wrestlers stayed with the St. Louis Wrestling Club's promoters, Matysik soon began filling his stable with some very reputable grapplers. On June 18, 1983, he held the first program under the auspices of his new company. Though the powers that be did their best to block Larry's access to the established stars of the day (just as Packs had done to Muchnick), Matysik

King Kong (a.k.a. Bruiser) Brody

had developed connections and relationships to the point where he was able to stage an eight-bout bill that featured the likes of "King Kong" Brody, Bob Sweetan, Tully Blanchard, Spike Huber, Angelo and Lanny Poffo, and Randy Savage. The question soon became whether both organizations could survive. Was there enough talent to promote quality matches that would draw fans? Over the long term, which promoter would win control of the territory? Or would there soon be someone else?

MAT MOMENTS

IS IT "BRUISER" BRODY OR "KING KONG" BRODY? In St. Louis, he was labeled "King Kong" because Sam Muchnick felt there were too many wrestlers that had ties to the "Bruiser" moniker—Bruiser Bob Sweetan, Dick the Bruiser, and even Nick the Bruiser, to name a few.

George Abel interviews Nick the Bruiser (a.k.a. Chester Bernard).
COURTESY OF ST. LOUIS MEDIA HISTORY FOUNDATION

TV BATTLES

WITH MATYSIK AND MICKEY GARAGIOLA no longer appearing on the St. Louis Wrestling Club's Chase program and the St. Louis Wrestling Club's promoters facing heavy competition, Larry struck a deal with St. Louis's newest independent television station, KDNL Channel 30, for a wrestling program that would air at 5 p.m. on Saturday evenings. Billed as "the new era of wrestling in St. Louis," Matysik's show hit the airwaves on August 6, 1983, in direct

competition with the St. Louis Wrestling Club's *Wrestling at the Chase*, which was shown later on Saturday evenings on KPLR-TV—at least initially. Larry's show began drawing viewers, while *Wrestling at the Chase* was in a tailspin owing to the changing environment of St. Louis's televised wrestling. Jack Adkisson (a.k.a. wrestler Fritz Von Erich), the leader of Dallas's NWA World Class Wrestling Association territory, had launched a new syndicated television program, *World Class Wrestling*, that began airing at the same time as *Wrestling at the Chase* on television sets across the St. Louis region. In fact, looking through television guides of 1983, wrestling shows were popping up all over the expanding cable television networks' programming. Stations like USA, WTBS, and other cable networks were televising nearly 10 hours of matches each week. The product had become diluted.

In response to the competition and falling ratings, Ted Koplar and the KPLR-TV team began talking with Matysik about coming back to his roots. Across the country, wrestling territories began to fall

Mickey Garagiola (left) and Larry Matysik are reunited as the commentators for the all-new "St. Louis Wrestling" on KDNL-TV, Channel 30, Saturday at 5 p.m. beginning Aug. 6. The personable pair previously worked together for better than eleven years.

Larry and Mickey move to KDNL Channel 30.
COURTESY OF BOB GARAGIOLA

Jack Adkisson (a.k.a. Fritz Von Erich)
COURTESY OF GETTY IMAGES

under the onrush of the national expansion. Larry's promotion operations, along with many older, larger, and more established organizations, collapsed as the last vestiges of the original National Wrestling Alliance were being wiped away. Matysik's St. Louis Wrestling Enterprises offered one final card at the Checkerdome on October 29, 1983. With Muchnick in retirement, the old guard of St. Louis wrestling had fallen, and the face of professional wrestling was now Vince McMahon, whose father, Vince Sr., and grandfather Jess had been longtime players in professional wrestling promotions in the NWA's northeast territories.

Verne Gagne, Vincent McMahon Sr., and Bruno Sammartino
COURTESY OF WIKIMEDIA COMMONS

Matysik's St. Louis Wrestling Enterprises promotions
COURTESY OF BOB GARAGIOLA

NEWSLETTER

Thursday, August 4, 1983

GREATER ST. LOUIS WRESTLING ENTERPRISES — Price Per Copy 75c

Page One

KDNL-TV 30 and KSHE-95 Welcome Wrestling Aug. 19

Dome Features Offer Action

ROMER

"King Kong" Brody knows he cannot afford to blow up again as he did July 22. Running out of control would create too many vulnerable spots for Toru Tanaka to attack Aug. 19 at The Checkerdome.

Royal Winner Huber, Adrian Adonis Clash; Tanaka Faces Brody

Excitement in excess is certain when Prof. Toru Tanaka confronts "King Kong" Brody and Adrian Adonis clashes with "Spike" Huber in the double main event at The Checkerdome Friday, Aug. 19.

Brody and Tanaka both feel they have a score to settle. On July 22 the two were on opposite sides of a wild tag team melee that ended when Brody was disqualified for tossing Tanaka over the top rope.

The bell did not, however, end the mayhem. So enraged was Brody that he went after Tanaka outside the ring. The two had a tremendous donnybrook, which also involved Tanaka's partner, Nikolai Volkoff.

Still, trouble between Tanaka and Brody had not ended. In the spine-tingling two-ring Battle Royal which closed the July 22 bill, Tanaka and Brody again found themselves butting heads.

In the first ring, Tanaka and Volkoff teamed to pitch Brody out. In the second ring, Brody became entangled with Tanaka and both were bumped over the ropes by the charging Volkoff. Another skirmish ensued on the floor before referees restored order.

Thus, Brody is straining at the leash to get after Tanaka. And the wily Japanese master of Oriental combat can-
(Continued on Page 4, Column 1)

Thesz Returns Home

All-time mat great Lou Thesz is coming home Friday, Aug. 19, at The Checkerdome.

A native of St. Louis, Thesz is going to be the special referee for the tussle between world title claimant Adrian Adonis and Battle Royal king "Spike" Huber. Thesz owned the gold belt some 18 years.

Lou Thesz

IT'S NOT BUSINESS AS USUAL ANYMORE

JUST LIKE THE CHANGES that took place in the sport in the 1920s and the 1940s, the 1980s saw wrestling once more at a crossroads. American society was entering a new era driven by the evolution of computers, video games, and cable television. The latter also came with a new and profitable opportunity known as pay-per-view. Just as vaudeville brought a brisker pace to theater and society in the 1920s, fans in the 1980s wanted wrestling matches that had the fast pace and explosiveness of the video era. The 1980s were definitely not like the 1950s. It wasn't just five television channels to watch anymore. It was now hundreds of stations 24 hours a day, all competing for viewership in an era of sensationalism not just in newsrooms but across basic programs as well. Professional wrestling was no exception. Everything got turned up a notch or two in order to grab the audience's attention.

Mighty Atom and
Cowboy Bradley in
November 1970

Bobby the Brain Heenan and Dick the Bruiser about to give Black Jack Lanza a little ride

For decades, Sam Muchnick's philosophies and leadership had been quite simple.[14] Professional wrestling should be more sport and less carnival. Matches should not insult the audience's intelligence. Sam had always tried to avoid the theatrics of adding women, little people, and tag teams to his cards. He didn't want the sensationalism they added. In time, Muchnick began adopting them in his programs more as a special attraction rather than on a regular basis. Only when he knew a particular undercard could be perceived as weak would he include any of the three to the program to add some pizazz. He wanted wrestling cards based on athleticism and brawn. In Sam's view, wrestling was simply magic—a "mesmerizing illusion."

Sure, there always were and always would be outspoken doubters of the genuineness of the sport, but as Muchnick noted, it didn't impact the throngs of crowds who would come by the thousands to watch professional wrestling here in St. Louis and across the nation. Sam always remained cautious and didn't want to give critics any more material. Sam wanted matches to be believable. They should express the real physicality of the sport and not provide a stage for

Penny Banner putting a finishing move on her opponent

COURTESY OF NICK REDNOUR

MAT
MOMENTS

BOB'S BIG GAFFE—Throughout his storied career, Bob Costas has been a class act loved by fans, athletes, and ownership. But there was one time in St. Louis when he rubbed Sam Muchnick the wrong way. While professional wrestling was not always high on the pyramid of sports talk on KMOX's *Sports Open Line*, Sam would occasionally call in to discuss an upcoming wrestling promotion. While hosting the show one night and getting the details from Sam on the different grapplers who would be appearing in matches later that week, Bob became Dorothy Gale with her dog Toto pulling back the curtain in *The Wizard of Oz* to expose the man pulling the strings.

As Sam wrapped up the preview of his wrestling card, Bob noted that he had a conflicting commitment and would not be at the match. He should have stopped there. Instead, without fully thinking, Bob "pulled back the curtain" by asking the question: "Can you let us know the winners now since I won't be there to see them?" Unsurprisingly, Sam was not amused.

Bob Costas, Dutch Snyder, and Mickey Garagiola at a wrestling match at the Checkerdome where Costas was providing a live feed for KMOX radio

COURTESY OF BOB GARAGIOLA

little wrestlers to run between referees' legs or for other wrestlers to spend more camera time out of the ring than inside of it. Thus wrestling was at a crossroads with the 1980s' new generation of promoters led by men such as Vince McMahon. Instead of old-style pure athleticism, this new look of wrestling was built on what some called scripted goofiness that used more sex, melodrama, and flashy pyrotechnics than just muscle and brawn. Former champion Lou Thesz called it "a clown act, a circus, with no dignity."[15] During his decades of leadership, Muchnick had kept promoters from drifting too far away from his philosophy. With Sam gone and the times changing, professional wrestling would soon change dramatically. McMahon had a big budget, big ideas, and a big stage. His brand was taking hold and winning over fans during the "decade of greed." At the same time that Ted Koplar and Matysik were negotiating to move Larry from KNDL-TV back to his old seat at KPLR-TV, Koplar

Mr. Fuji is put in an opponent's headlock at the ropes.
COURTESY OF GETTY IMAGES

FOR CLARITY, MCMAHON'S PROFESSIONAL WRESTLING empire's name no longer falls under the WWF or World Wrestling Federation moniker following a 2002 lawsuit filed and won by the World Wildlife Fund, which also used WWF as its trademark. As a result, McMahon's company changed its business name to become World Wrestling Entertainment Inc., or WWE for short. Originally named Capitol Wrestling Corporation (CWC), it had changed its name to the World Wide Wrestling Federation (WWWF) in 1963 before becoming the World Wrestling Federation.

Vince McMahon
COURTESY OF GETTY IMAGES

THE RESURGENCE OF THE NWA. For nearly 25 years, the NWA was led by Sam Muchnick. After his tenure ended in 1975, there would be 22 leadership changes through the year 2017, as its promotions operated in the shadows of the WWE. In May 2017, former Smashing Pumpkins lead singer Billy Corgan purchased the NWA, including its name, rights, trademarks, and championship belts.[16] In the ensuing years, Corgan and his team's promotions have continued to work to bring the NWA back to prominence centered around heavyweight champion Nick Aldis and their ventures with FITE TV.

NWA owner Billy Corgan and Nick Aldis
IMAGE COURTESY OF NICK ALDIS

and McMahon were also negotiating an alliance that would soon replace the St. Louis Wrestling Club's product on Koplar's network with McMahon's new Worldwide Wrestling Federation (WWF) programming. Despite the cynics, McMahon and his product succeeded in revolutionizing professional wrestling, which is still going strong on television and in arenas across the nation four decades later.

THE END IS NEAR

WITH THE AGREEMENT between Koplar and McMahon in hand, KPLR-TV ended its relationship with the St. Louis Wrestling Club in September 1983. In addition to his network, Koplar still had his epic location, which was always an attractive and well-known backdrop for the sport. McMahon's program would become the last hurrah of wrestling filmed in the Khorassan Room of the Chase Hotel. Unlike the original program produced by the Koplar company in conjunction with Muchnick, this new arrangement with McMahon and the WWF had KPLR-TV paying for the rights to air the programming. Beginning on December 27, 1983, matches were once again taped at the hotel and cut into episodes billed as *Wrestling at the Chase*. These matches interjected some new names to the local wrestling scene including the first WWF matches of Gene Okerlund and Hulk Hogan. These shows began airing in early January 1984. A month later, subsequent matches took place and were filmed at Kiel Auditorium before one final taping was set for the Chase Hotel on September 28, 1984. That show aired at 11 a.m. on October 21, 1984. After that, all that would be shown were syndicated matches until the program was finally canceled in 1985. The ringside bell inside the Chase Hotel would ring no more!

The program moved into the KPLR-TV studio to film the matches.
COURTESY OF MERCANTILE LIBRARY

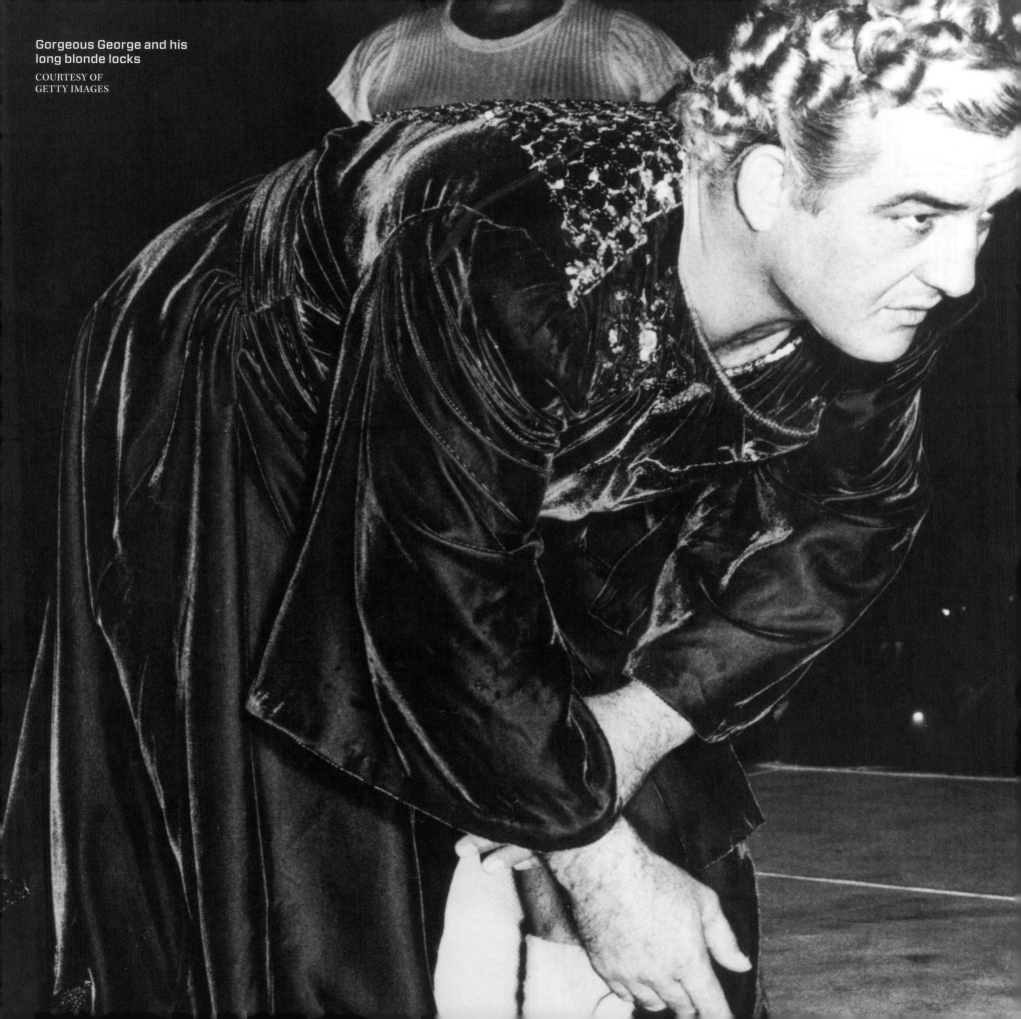

Gorgeous George and his
long blonde locks

PART! 3

★★★★★★★★★★★★★★★★★★★★★★★★

★★★★★★

THE SUCCESS OF THE SHOW WAS SIMPLE

★★★★★★

COURTESY OF RICH NOFFKE

The Fabulous Moolah

ST. LOUIS WRESTLING CLUB

UPPER BALCONY

SEC. 16 ROW B SEAT 4

DECEMBER
4
1970

FRIDAY - 8:30 P. M.

KIEL AUDITORIUM
1400 MARKET ST.

ADMISSION
$1.50
NO REFUNDS

SAM MUCHNICK

25th ANNIVERSARY AS PROMOTER

IT WAS ALL ABOUT SAM'S WRESTLERS

THE SUCCESS OF *WRESTLING AT THE CHASE* would not have been possible without Sam Muchnick's wrestling promotions. The wrestlers in his stable provided the necessary foundation to ensure the strength of the program's long-term success. It was the physical skill, charm, and actions of these men and women that attracted fans back to the program week after week, year after year—and soon those years turned into decades. These were not just once-a-month or once-a-year matches for fans to watch. There would be another match to promote and quench the same fans' thirst in just seven days. Most of the men and women who were now performing before the KPLR-TV cameras had been on the wrestling circuit around the country. Their names were familiar, and many had performed in St. Louis multiple times at either the Arena or Kiel Auditorium matches. Interestingly, these grapplers were only being paid between $75 and $100 a match plus travel expenses before heading off to the next town and their next set of matches. But it was the exposure and Muchnick's marketing that came with the *Wrestling at the Chase* program that kept these wrestlers coming back to St. Louis year after year. So how do you keep the promotions fresh and keep the fans coming back?

There was something different about these matches at the Chase. Beyond the opulence of the venue, there was the proximity to the action. While the Khorassan Room was large enough for a regal social ball, it was no arena or auditorium in size or capacity. Ringside fans heard every grunt, threat, and slam while also getting an occasional misting of sweat or spit. At home the television set brought the action so close it was even better than ringside. It was like you were inside the ring, and the wrestlers were simply the same distance away as the television set. It was easy for fans to be sucked in and form a bond with their favorite wrestlers.

Muchnick and King Kong Brody

As a heel, Jessie "The Body" Ventura wrestled using the motto "Win if you can, lose if you must, but always cheat!"

Dory Funk Jr. puts a move on King Kong Brody.

HEELS, FACES, AND A FEW TWEENERS

WHILE THEIR PHYSICAL SIZE and athleticism was greater than those of most fans, the individual wrestlers' personas were even larger. In the programs nearly 25-year run, thousands of men and women climbed through *Wrestling at the Chase*'s ropes to enter the ring. As a wrestler's name was announced, fans ringside and television viewers everywhere immediately knew in which camp the grappler belonged. In the sport of

Nature Boy Ric Flair's robe-attired entrance to the ring
COURTESY OF GETTY IMAGES

Hulk Hogan engages the crowd on the way to the ring.
COURTESY OF GETTY IMAGES

professional wrestling, these warriors were divided into two camps: the "heels" and the "faces." The heels were there to be booed and jeered. They were wrestling's bad boys, portrayed as villains and antagonists to their righteous opponents from the faces' camp. The faces were the heroic protagonists in the ring and were bathed with cheers and applause. Inside the ropes, it was a timeless battle of good versus evil—with the hope that good would prevail—at least most of the time.

82

King Kong Brody takes on the war-painted Kamala, the Ugandan Giant.

Dick the Bruiser in the crowd outside the ring as announcer George Abel looks on and Mickey Garagiola steers clear and peeks out behind the screen on the left

COURTESY OF ST. LOUIS MEDIA HISTORY FOUNDATION

Within the love-hate drama of every match, the heels' actions focused on spurring fans hatred toward them as the foil of the face. This came in many ways. It sometimes began with the theatrical flair of their very entrance into the ring. Gorgeous George made the best of his outlandish entrance, strutting along a royal red carpet to the music of "Pomp and Circumstance," wearing an extraordinary purple robe and accompanied by beautiful escorts. Ric Flair would carry on that same tradition decades later. At other times, a heel would stage his or her act by wearing a mask, face paint, or some type of over-the-top outfit— generally "bad guy" black in color. Often the heels would exhibit contempt toward the ringside audience or television commentators. At other times, these antagonistic wrestlers would grab an announcer's microphone and deliver a verbal soliloquy on their own greatness while demeaning the pathetic nature of their opponent. There would be times when a heel not associated with the match of the moment would disregard all rules and rush in from the locker room, climb into the ring, and save a fellow heel from near-certain defeat. Then there would be other times when the wrestling heels would leave the ring to continue the fight or simply refresh themselves with a fan's beer or bratwurst. It was in this context that Mickey Garagiola delivered one of his best zingers about the battles outside the ring: "If another head gets bounced off this table, it will have more hits than Stan Musial. And he had 3000!"[17]

Gorgeous George Rogers with one of his lavish robes

COURTESY OF WIKIMEDIA COMMONS

MAT
MOMENTS

WHILE THERE WERE RULES, rules are meant to be broken if you are good enough. In his book *Wrestling at the Chase*, Larry Matysik gave an example of how the rules were not always followed while describing a 1978 tag-team match when Ted DiBiase and his partner Rocky Johnson took on Dick Murdoch and Bob Sweetan.[18] Early in the match, Murdoch pitched Ted from the ring and followed him to the floor. 'No two men on the floor!' barked Dick, punching Ted in the jaw. 'Don't use furniture,' he then said, slamming DiBiase's head into the table where Mickey and I were sitting. 'Stay away from the equipment!' he screamed as he took the long camera cable and wrapped it around Ted's throat to choke him. DiBiase was positive Dick was going to get him fired. Then Murdoch whispered, 'Now it's your turn kid.' Dick turned the tables and had Ted do everything he'd just done. The scrap ended as a no-contest, when Rocky and Dick were both counted out while fighting on the announcer's platform. 'We went up the steps and I was scared to death that I'd be fired,' Ted said. 'Sam came right up to me and my heart just sank. Then he smiled, shook my hand, and told me. 'Great match, kid! Way to go.' I caught Murdoch's eye and he just winked.'

Dick Murdoch

Ted DiBiase

Dick Murdoch explaining things to Larry Matysik

Baron Von Raschke slamming Harley Race outside the ring

special St. Louis was when he reminded them before every match: "St. Louis is the only town that doesn't have to pay to be on television, so keep it clean but tough." He also instilled the rule: "No two men on the floor at the same time. Don't use the furniture. Stay away from the equipment. Don't get us kicked off TV."[19]

Sam had allowed the rules to be broken because they were stars. His edicts were meant for the new and inexperienced guys to ensure they stayed in line. But that doesn't mean Muchnick didn't have respect for the newbies. In a 1975 column in *Wrestling News*, Sam stated:

> "I had no favorites. To me the lowliest preliminary boy is as valuable as the biggest star and gate magnet. Before you get main eventers, you have to have the understudies and they, eventually, if they have the right kind of ability, graduate to the top rung. I have always appreciated the work of the men in the earlier matches as much as I did those who were in the features and received the big money."

Breaking the rules or cheating during the matches added spice to the match and drew a loud response from the audience. There were other times when a heel would fail to abide by the referee's commands or maybe even turn against the man in the striped shirt and engage in illegal hits, pull an opponent's hair or ears, or illegally use the ropes to gain leverage against his foe. It could be even more dastardly when a heel would use an illegal weapon while the referee wasn't looking, be it a bottle or a strip of sandpaper pulled out of his trunks and applied to his disabled opponent's face. It was pure artistic and athletic theater at its best. In the end, there was an unlimited variety of dirty tricks that a wrestler from the heel camp could pull in order to keep the engaged fans on the edge of their seats just waiting to see what would happen next.

Despite all of the theatrics, wrestler Baron Von Raschke notes, "Sam actually had rules that the referees had to enforce. At the *Wrestling at the Chase* tapings, the booker would go over the rules before the show. You better follow those rules or you were short lived for return shows." And Sam would never let the wrestlers forget how

Buddy Rogers

Not following the rules was in stark contrast to the perceived holiness of the faces. Simply put, the face was a "good guy," the good-looking knight in shining armor whose purpose on the match's card was to be loved and cheered by an adoring crowd while winning the match with his strength and skill—totally the antithesis of the heel they would be wrestling. In fact, the term "face" within the sport is short for "baby face" as a descriptor of their looks. To most of the fans, faces resembled the good kid in school, always doing what the teacher asked so as to please everyone. In this case, they followed the referee's directions and respected the fans in the audience. This made them the favorites of most fans, or at least that was how it was perceived in the script. They played by the rules and generally never cheated and at the same time gained crowd favor and sympathy for having to endure the cheating of the heels. And in most instances, the wrestling face would regain just enough balance and strength to rally to victory just when defeat seemed inevitable.

That is not to say that all fans were always aligned with the faces, nor did faces always win. There would even be matches—for example, when Gene Kiniski went against Killer Kowalski, Dick the Bruiser faced Fritz Von Erich, or Dory Funk Jr. wrestled Pat O'Connor—that featured heel versus heel or face versus face. There was an extra level of excitement for the fans during these matches. Everyone wanted to find out who would come out on top of the totem pole in each of the two camps. Then there were always those fans who no matter what, rooted for wrestlers from the dark side because they just didn't like the goody-goody of a face wrestler's script. It's just like life's roles in school or in social circles but played out in a ring in front of thousands of people with the heel wrestler at times delivering a smackdown on the goody-goody face—something that fans could never do in school. All of this just strengthened the ties between the fans and the grapplers.

The battle lines were not always black versus white. There were instances through the life of *Wrestling at the Chase* where a wrestler went from one camp to the other. Ric Flair for one was perceived as a face but often adopted actions associated with a heel—or was it simply perceived by the fans as a situation where he was giving his combatant a taste of his own medicine? In instances where a heel continually received more cheers from the audience than his opponent in matches, promoters might rescript the wrestler's role to turn him into a face or have him engage in even more dastardly acts in the ring that would place him more firmly into the heel camp. Often these characters are referred to as "tweeners," to reflect their shifting roles. That was the beauty of professional wrestling in its golden years. It kept the fans enthralled and engaged, and there was no better place for it to play out than in the ring inside the Khorassan Room of the Chase Hotel.

MUST BE THE NEW MATH! While most fans were lock, stock, and barrel believers and die-hard followers of televised professional wrestling, there were always those disbelievers. One such set of skeptics wrote to the *Post-Dispatch*'s Television Letter Box in March 1953 questioning the oddity of these matches. "My husband and I enjoy quite a number of programs during the week, including the Saturday night wrestling matches. That is until we added two and two and got the right answer. One Saturday evening we saw the light after asking ourselves why the last wrestling match always ended precisely at 11 o'clock. Then we attempted to name one legitimate sporting event which could be timed so perfectly. The answer is none. At any rate, the actors who portray wrestlers should be congratulated for their ability to end the exhibition at the correct time without ever missing the cue." The letter was signed "EX-WRESTLING FANS."

Ric Flair

89

PART 4

I ♥ KING KONG BRODY

THE BIGGEST STARS WHO SHONE ON *WRESTLING* AT THE CHASE

A barefooted Antonino Rocca takes control.

The Great Togo

THEY WRESTLED HERE

SO WHO WERE THESE WRESTLERS who climbed into that ring week after week, and what camp were they from? It was not the same grapplers wrestling every week as you would have with baseball teams playing the same lineup game after game. Week after week, Sam Muchnick used a large stable of veterans, including current and former champions, while also introducing new talent to keep his weekly matches fresh and relevant. Since it has been over sixty years since the first wrestler climbed into the Chase Hotel's ring, many have passed, but their legacy remains. When *Wrestling at the Chase* came on the air in 1959, the top-ranked wrestlers rated by *Boxing Illustrated/Wrestling News* at the end of 1958 were:

1. Dick Hutton (NWA World Champion)
2. Whipper Billy Watson
3. Killer Kowalski
4. Buddy Rogers
5. Pat O'Connor
6. Pepper Gomez
7. Enrique Torres
8. Verne Gagne
9. Édouard Carpentier
10. Antonino Rocca

Édouard Carpentier doing a number on Baron Von Raschke

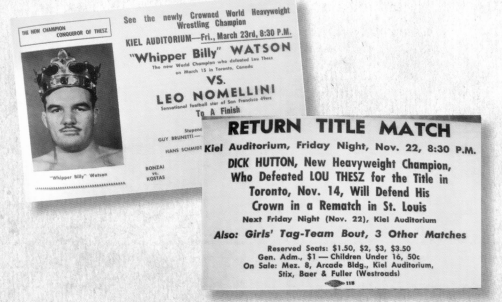

See the newly Crowned World Heavyweight Wrestling Champion

KIEL AUDITORIUM—Fri., March 23rd, 8:30 P.M.

"Whipper Billy" WATSON
The new World Champion who defeated Lou Thesz on March 15 in Toronto, Canada

VS.

LEO NOMELLINI
Sensational football star of San Francisco 49ers

To A Finish

THE NEW CHAMPION CONQUEROR OF THESZ

"Whipper Billy" Watson

Stupendo...
GUY BRUNETTI —
HANS SCHMIDT

BONZAI
vs.
KOSTAS

RETURN TITLE MATCH

Kiel Auditorium, Friday Night, Nov. 22, 8:30 P.M.

DICK HUTTON, New Heavyweight Champion, **Who Defeated LOU THESZ for the Title in** Toronto, Nov. 14, Will Defend His Crown in a Rematch in St. Louis

Next Friday Night (Nov. 22), Kiel Auditorium

Also: Girls' Tag-Team Bout, 3 Other Matches

Reserved Seats: $1.50, $2, $3, $3.50
Gen. Adm., $1 — Children Under 16, 50c
On Sale: Mez. 8, Arcade Bldg., Kiel Auditorium,
Stix, Baer & Fuller (Westroads)
118

While not listed in the top 10 of 1958, longtime St. Louisan, fan favorite, and former world champion Lou Thesz would be back on the list within a year. This book cannot highlight everyone who entered the ring or every match that took place. But there are some who stand out and deserve special attention. In putting together the following biographical sketches of many of the most popular men and women who wrestled at the Chase, the list should start with Thesz. Not only was he a world champion, but he was also involved in the early days of professional wrestling in St. Louis dating back to the feud and spin-off of Sam Muchnick from Tom Packs.

Viadek "Killer" Kowalski lets out a holler as the feet of Pat O'Connor land against his face.

Pat O'Connor swings wrestling champion Lou Thesz through the air during their match.
COURTESY OF GETTY IMAGES

LOU THESZ was not born in St. Louis but is perceived as a native of the town, having moved to the river city at an early age. Young Aloysius Martin Thesz would go by Lou and grow up to be a six-time world champion. He held the NWA title three times for a combined period of over ten years—more than any other wrestler in history. Perhaps Lou's wrestling skills came naturally. His father, Martin, was a Hungarian immigrant who had been the national Greco-Roman champion in his homeland. While dabbling in various forms of wrestling and boxing, Lou dropped out of high school at fourteen. Through his father's ties, he kept training in freestyle wrestling at St. Louis's Cleveland High School. That preparation and pedigree soon had young Lou winning city and regional tournaments while catching the eye of St. Louis promoter Tom Packs.

Lou Thesz

Packs sent Lou to train under George Tragos, a former Greek Olympic wrestler who at one time served as the University of Missouri's wrestling coach. Thesz made his professional wrestling debut at the age of 16 in 1932. Five years later, he was one of the St. Louis territory's biggest stars. In the last days of 1937, he defeated Everett Marshall to win the American Wrestling Association world heavyweight championship. He was the youngest champion in history, and this was the first of his many titles. After a series of defeats, he won the title again in 1939, defeating Marshall once more, and in 1948 he won it again by defeating Bill Longson. That same year, he was awarded the unified title of the National Wrestling Alliance when Orville Brown succumbed to injuries from an auto accident. In 1952, Thesz continued his championship unification matches by defeating Baron Michele Leone for the California world

heavyweight title. After losing the unified title to Whipper Billy Watson in 1956, he soon won it back. The next year he was injured in a match with Édouard Carpentier. The NWA rules would not officially recognize this as a defeat because Thesz stopped the match due to a legitimate injury, but some promoters tried to give Edouard claim to the title. Thesz healed from his injuries and went to Japan as the first wrestler to defend a title there. He faced off against Rikidouzan, a Korean-Japanese wrestler, in a series of bouts that would popularize professional wrestling in that nation. Shortly thereafter, Thesz dropped the title and went on a financially lucrative barnstorming tour across Japan and Europe. He came out of retirement in 1963 and won back the championship from Buddy Rogers at the age of 46. He would hold the title another three years before losing to Gene Kiniski. Thesz would win one last title in 1978 in Mexico when he won the inaugural Universal Wrestling Alliance heavyweight championship at the age of 62. For seven decades, Thesz had performed in professional wrestling matches around the world and was often a regular on *Wrestling at the Chase.* Lou Thesz was not only the major wrestler of this golden age but was also a promoter and would go on to partner with Sam Muchnick to develop the greatest wrestling syndicate of the time. Thesz passed away on April 9, 2002, at the age of 86 due to complications from heart surgery.

BUDDY ROGERS was the premier wrestler who helped put Sam Muchnick on the map. Born to German immigrant parents in 1921, Herman Gustav Rohde Jr. changed his name to Buddy Rogers as he rose to the top of wrestling's leaderboard while also becoming one of early televised wrestling's biggest stars. Over his career, Rogers was a 13-time world champion across different territories while also holding the top championships in both the NWA and WWWF (later changed to WWF and then WWE). Rogers was in fact the inaugural heavyweight champion of the latter when he took the belt on April 11, 1963.

With his charisma, athletic physique, and bleached blonde hair, Rogers was initially promoted by his manager as "Nature Guy." That soon evolved into "Nature Boy," a moniker that would later be adopted by other wrestlers like Ric Flair. Adding to that persona and brand, Rogers developed his own signature move, the figure-four leg lock. In his memoir, *Hooker*, Lou Thesz wrote that Rogers:

> "was also one of the first guys to rely a lot on what we called 'flying' moves in the ring— body slams, dropkicks,

piledrivers, ricochets off the ropes into his opponent; action moves that are all commonplace today. All of those moves were in use before Rogers came along, but they were used sparingly. Most of the wrestling prior to Rogers's emergence was done on the mat. Rogers was the first to use flying moves in quantity, staying off the mat, and the style was so popular with the fans that other wrestlers, including me, followed his lead."[20]

Rogers joined Sam Muchnick's ranks during the promoter's feud with Tom Packs and the latter's prize wrestler, Lou Thesz. The two grapplers eventually wrestled to a draw in one of the premier events pitting the two St. Louis promoters. With rising star Rogers in his stable, Muchnick won the battle between the two promoters and would go on to lead the national wrestling enterprise. Rogers won the NWA national heavyweight championship from Pat O'Connor in 1961. After many challenges and other matches over the next several years, Rogers lost a title fight to Thesz in 1963 that directly led promoters Toots Mondt and Vince McMahon Sr. to withdraw from the NWA and form the World Wide Wrestling Federation (WWWF, now WWE) with Rogers as their new champion. Nature Boy Rogers continued to wrestle all the way up to his death in June 1992 when he suffered a stroke.

Buddy Rogers
COURTESY OF GETTY IMAGES

Buddy Rogers in action

WRESTLING
TONIGHT AT 8:30
KIEL AUDITORIUM
Championship Match
DICK   PAT
HUTTON vs. **O'CONNOR**
World Champion   No. 1 Challenger
One Fall to a Finish!!!
HANDICAP BOUT—Gene Kiniski
vs. Lou Plummer & Chest Bernard
GIRLS' MATCH—Penny Banner vs.
Lorraine Johnston.
4-MAN TAG TEAM BOUT—
Joe Tangaro and Ray Stevens
vs. Don Fargo and Stu Gibson
And One Other Thrilling Bout
GEN. $1 On Sale 7:00 Tonight
ADM.   At Kiel Auditorium
            Children Under 16—60c
Reserved seats on sale Mezzanine B,
Arcade Bldg., Kiel Auditorium and
Stix, Baer & Fullers Westroads
Store. For information phone GE.
6-4400.
Sam Muchnick, Promoter

June 1961's "match of the century"

UNFORGETTABLE NIGHT IN COMISKEY PARK, CHICAGO

June 30, 1961 - Buddy Rogers defeats Pat O'Connor to win the Heavyweight Championship of the World.

Attendance: 38,622   —   Promoted by Fred Kohler and Vince McMahon   —   Receipts: $141,345.00

Pat O'Connor, the wrestler from Down Under, is being tossed up and over by Hans Hermann.
COURTESY OF GETTY IMAGES

Pat O'Connor
COURTESY OF
GETTY IMAGES

PAT O'CONNOR was also a mainstay of the program as a wrestler, referee, and sometimes television commentator who came to the program via his birthplace in New Zealand. He was simultaneously an American Wrestling Association and National Wrestling Alliance heavyweight world champion. Pat won the latter title for the first time in 1959 when he defeated Dick Hutton. O'Connor lost his title to Buddy Rogers in June 1961 in what was dubbed the match of the century at Chicago's Comiskey Park. That match set a record for attendance (38,622) and ticket revenues ($148,000) that would last for over two decades. While a regular grappler in St. Louis's venues and at the Chase, O'Connor took part in Sam Muchnick's last professional program on January 1, 1982. Pat had become one of the owners of the St. Louis Wrestling Club, and the day after Sam's retirement Pat partnered with Verne Gagne, Harley Race, and Bob Geigel to purchase Muchnick's full wrestling territory and operations. Pat passed away days shy of his 66th birthday in 1990.

The Bruiser wearing number 72 is a formidable presence in the middle of the Green Bay Packers team photo.

DICK THE BRUISER: With all due respect to the various champions and fantastic talent that worked in St. Louis over the years, Dick the Bruiser might be the wrestler most associated with *Wrestling at the Chase*. His first match on *Wrestling at the Chase* was January 19, 1963. Former St. Louis Wrestling Club promoter Larry Matysik described the Bruiser best when he said, "Bruiser was the same person inside the ring as he was outside the ring. There was no character or personality switch." Born Richard Afflis, in Lafayette, Indiana, he was built like a tank and played football for one season at Purdue and was named to the All–Big Ten team before leaving for the University of Nevada. When not playing football at the latter school, he was a bouncer at Harold's Club in Reno. His first professional sport was football, with the Green Bay Packers signing him to play in 1951. Bruiser was no great star at football, but he was a good, consistent player. His Green Bay teammates nicknamed him "Bruiser" for his style. A blow to the Adam's apple gave him his raspy, rough voice. He left football in the mid-1950s for wrestling "to make a better buck." With his rough tactics and reputation for annoying fans, he was a natural as a bad guy. He would tear down signs and break pens of

Dick the Bruiser working on Black Jack Lanza

Wrestling

ST. LOUIS WRESTLING CLUB — Subscription $1.00 per Season—Single Copy 15c — Page One

Saturday, August 14 1965

Season Opener at Kiel, Aug. 20

DORY FUNK SR. AND JR.

DICK "THE BRUISER"

Two Features

"Bruiser," Funks Clash In Handicap Fracas; Snyder vs. Von Erich

COURTESY OF IRENE MUELLER

Dick the Bruiser putting a little extra on his finish with King Kong Brody

Dick the Bruiser—the wrestler everyone loved to hate!

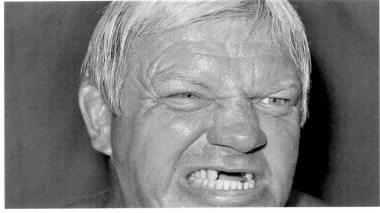

autograph seekers, and he loved to cause crowd disturbances. In his prime in the mid-1960s, he earned $100,000 a year. Bruiser wrestled in front of mainly sellout crowds at Kiel Auditorium. His top opponents were Lou Thesz, Fritz Von Erich, Cowboy Bob Ellis, Johnny Valentine, and Pat O'Connor. Bruiser was famous for often grabbing drinks at ringside from tables where patrons were watching the match. He would get a beer from a fan, pour it over his own head after the match, and run out into the lobby. His trademark scowl, crew cut, and gravel voice helped earn him the prime-time marquee billing as "the world's most dangerous wrestler." In the late 1960s, Bruiser started to wrestle other heels, and his popularity increased. A feud with Black Jack Lanza and Bobby Heenan gained national attention and helped turn him into a fan favorite. The character switch was not planned. The fans had made the decision. The wrestler most fans feared yet cheered passed away at the age of 62 in November 1991, due to a ruptured blood vessel while lifting weights. Once you saw him in the ring, you never forgot him.

Dick the Bruiser

RIC FLAIR: This fantastic performer and wrestler can easily be included in a very short list of the all-time best in the history of professional wrestling. There are many facts to support this claim. His career began in 1972 and spanned over 35 years. He was trained by former champion Verne Gagne and quickly rose to become one of the top stars when he won his first television title in the Mid-Atlantic territory. Flair was involved in a plane crash in 1975 (along with Johnny Valentine), and he suffered a broken back. His career was nearly finished. He managed to bounce back a little over a year later, won another regional title, and joined Greg Valentine to capture a version of the world tag-team championship. Flair would climb to another level when he worked in St. Louis, and in particular on *Wrestling at the*

Chase. His use of the moniker "Nature Boy" soon erupted into a bitter feud with the original Nature Boy, Buddy Rogers.

From his first St. Louis main event on January 27, 1978, when he beat Dory Funk Jr., Flair was a headliner and box-office magnet. When he began his first reign as NWA champion in 1975, he proved to everyone in the business what St. Louis already knew. Whether grappling against David Von Erich or Ted DiBiase, Harley Race or Dick the Bruiser, King Kong Brody or Jack Brisco, Flair was the catalyst for the type of action that made St. Louis wrestling so special during a career that lasted all the way up to his retirement in 2012.

Flair's Nature Boy robe
COURTESY OF WIKIMEDIA COMMONS

Ric Flair

Flair for the win with referee Lee Warren

Larry Matysik with Ted DiBiase

Ted DiBiase

TED DIBIASE, who became known as the "Million Dollar Man," was a young wrestler who came to St. Louis during the last years of the program. He would go on to a stellar championship career as a solo grappler as well as a tag-team partner. And believe it or not, there was that one very special time that DiBiase became the only man ever crowned "Heavyweight Champion of the World" on the *Wrestling at the Chase* televised program.[21] Or was he?

MAT MOMENTS

MICKEY'S GOOF! On August 19, 1979, *Wrestling at the Chase* featured a tag-team match featuring Ted DiBiase and Paul Orndorff squaring off against world champion Harley Race and his partner "Bulldog" Bob Brown. As soon as the opening bell rang, fans knew this was going to be something special. It was a toe-to-toe struggle from the start, and as Mickey would later say, "they were pulling every stop out of the pan" . . . both inside and outside the ring. Brown had thrown DiBiase out of the ring and with a quick tag Race jumped on DiBiase, who was still on the outside, and the two began wrestling on the studio's concrete floor. After the referee finally got the match back in the ring, DiBiase surprised Race with a speedy back suplex drop that led to a quick pin of the champ. The crowd was in disbelief and screaming. No one was probably more excited than Mickey Garagiola, who jumped into the ring and declared to the shock of the entire wrestling world that "in 29 minutes and 14 seconds, the new world heavyweight champion, Ted DiBiase." Race was on his knees screaming, "no, Mickey, no." While the studio audience roared with excitement, thinking they had seen a title change, Mickey had forgotten that wrestling's rules do not permit a title change in a tag-team match, much less on a local televised program. In the end, that is what made Mickey so human and loveable. He was simply a fan caught up in the action and had made a mistake.

HARLEY RACE could be called the toughest, most durable wrestler of his time and likely for any period of time. Race was considered a top wrestler who could either brawl or simply use fundamental skills to defeat an opponent. His tenure (30-plus years) in the ring and his eight-time NWA world champion status puts Race in an elite class. Even though he may not be mentioned in the same breath as Lou Thesz, Pat O'Connor, or Ed "Strangler" Lewis, Race can be credited with adapting his style to that of his opponent or to the pace of a match. He was trained at age 16 by Kansas City promoter Gust Karras. Harley almost didn't have a career after he was involved in a horrible car accident. He refuted doctors who said he might never walk again and instead made them believers. He won a few regional titles early in his career and started to pick up momentum. He and partner Larry "The Ax" Hennig won the AWA world tag-team title four times. It was there that Race earned the reputation as a tough competitor. He jumped into the spotlight when he beat NWA champion Dory Funk Jr. in 1973. Jack Brisco won the title from Race just 57 days later, but that didn't stop Race. He kept winning titles (including the Missouri championship) and reclaimed the NWA championship in 1977 when he downed Terry Funk. The title switched hands in 1979 with Race losing to Dusty Rhodes, but Harley later took the gold belt back from Japanese star Giant Baba. The title would switch again a year later in

Harley Race in action
COURTESY OF WIKIMEDIA COMMONS

A young Harley Race

Tokyo, going back to Baba with Race regaining it a few days later. His status in Japan was Hall of Fame. His bouts in St. Louis and around the country made him even more popular with fans because of his willingness to wrestle almost anybody. Race's win over reigning champ Ric Flair in St. Louis in 1983 broke Lou Thesz's record for most NWA championships won by a single wrestler (seven). Race endured into the World Wrestling Federation in the mid-1980s. However, most fans will remember him for his glory days in the NWA, where he ruled as a tough guy, a longtime champion, and a fan favorite in St. Louis. Harley retired in 1990 and passed away on August 1, 2019, due to complications from lung cancer at the age of 76.

KING KONG (A.K.A. BRUISER) BRODY was a very popular wrestler in the later days of *Wrestling at the Chase*, who, like Dick the Bruiser, maintains a cult-like following across the region. After making his professional wrestling debut in 1973, Brody went on to develop a wrestling persona known for brutality and one in which he would occasionally go off script and hit or hurt an opponent during a match. If Brody was to be in the ring, the fans would fill the stands. In July 1988, he was stabbed to death in a locker room by a fellow wrestler during an alleged argument prior to a match in Puerto Rico. He was only 42 years old.

A six-foot eight-inch, three-hundred-pound "wild man"

Brody battling before a St. Louis crowd

Like his namesake King Kong, Brody holds his sweetheart like the ape held Fay Wray, high atop the Checkerdome sign.

Brody achieved a cult-like status.

COURTESY OF BOB GARAGIOLA

WILD BILL LONGSON was maybe the best and longest-reigning heel as a world champion in history, as well as one of the top drawing cards. Longson started his long career on the West Coast and almost didn't make it to St. Louis after suffering a broken back in 1937 in San Francisco. He emerged the next year wearing a mask and was named the Purple Shadow. Longson won three Pacific Coast titles. He moved to St. Louis in 1941 and became promoter Tom Packs's biggest drawing card. He won the NWA championship from Sandor Szabo on February 19, 1942. His battles with Orville Brown were memorable as well. He eventually lost the title to Yvon Robert in Montreal but reclaimed the championship from Bobby Managoff in St. Louis on February 19, 1943. He held the belt for four more years before being disqualified in a contest with Whipper Billy Watson on February 21, 1947, in a historic title match. In one of the best matches ever in St. Louis, Longson won the NWA title from Lou Thesz on November 21, 1947. After dropping the belt in 1948 but remaining popular with the fans, Longson retired and moved into the front office, promoting and booking talent for Sam Muchnick until 1977. Longson died December 10, 1982, in St. Louis at the age of 76.

Wild Bill Longson

Sports Pointers

Volume VII

No. M-6 Mezzanine Floor, Arcade Bldg.

St. Louis, Mo., Friday, September 10, 1948

Number 17

10

LONGSON AND TORRES IN RE-MATCH

MATDOM'S BIGGEST DRAWING CARD

Fans Demand Another Go Between Ex-Champ And Pugnacious "Mex"

St. Louis wrestling fans have been clamoring for such a bout for a long time, so insists Matchmaker Bill Nelson.

We are refering to the return finish bout between Enrique Torres, Sonora, Mexico, mat sensation, and Wild Bill Longson, former world champion. They will trade grips in a return finish bout on the Mississippi Valley Sports Club mat card Friday night, Sept. 10, at the air conditioned Kiel Auditorium.

First of five bouts will get under way at 8:30.

GET YOUR AUTOGRAPH

Get your Sports Pointers autographed wrestling fans! A mat star will greet you from 8 to 8:30 p. m. Friday, Sept.10, at the official table near Committee Room A in the 14th street foyer. There will be a wrestler of national renown on hand at all M.V.S.C. programs for the purpose of autographing your latest Sports Pointers. The time always, 8 to 8:30 p. m.

Wild Bill found Enrique a tough hombre in their initial meeting Friday night, August 27. The roughouse Mexican belted Longson out of the ring three times before he was disqualified by Referee Otto (Whitey) Brexler.

BOYS BECOME ENRAGED

Torres and his coach, Benny Ginzberg, became enraged following the verdict which by the way was rendered at the 11 minute, 10 second mark. The May-he-can went on to punch both Referee Brexler and Second Milo Occhi on the chin before the Missouri State Athletic Commission fined him $50 and suspended him indefinitely.

Upon peyment of his fine Torres personally apologized to both Brexler and Occhi and was put back in good standing by Charles Wingate Pian, chief deputy to Commissioner William Herring.

Longson is eager to meet the Bad Boy from the Land of Manana in the rematch, for he realizes he must get by Torres if he is ever to land another titular bout with Lou Thesz, present National Wrestling Association champion. Bill, though not the mat king, is still packin' 'em in throughout the country, especially in the Midwest, Texas, East and Canada.

Before his bout with Longson Torres won from Sky Hi Lee and Iron Man Talun, both in quick time, the latter victim lasting but 58 seconds.

WILD BILL LONGSON, FORMER CHAMPION

Autograph

MAT MOMENTS

SAM'S *WRESTLING AT THE CHASE* PAYOUTS: Sam Muchnick's spiral notebook of financial records reveals the payouts to his grapplers. The size of the payments was directly related to the pecking order of a wrestler's stature. Don't judge these amounts in today's terms. In looking back to 1978, these were pretty good sums of money for about an hour or so of work!

Wrestling at the Chase payouts

THURSDAY, APRIL 21st
KIEL AUDITORIUM
14th and Market Sts.

GENE KINISKI
vs.
COWBOY BOB ELLIS
TO A FINISH

— Man Tag Match

ALSO ON THIS STUPENDOUS PROGRAM —

6 MAN AUSTRALIAN TAG TEAM MATCH

RIP HAWK
ROCK HUNTER
KINJI SHIBUYA

VS.

RAY GORDON
WILBUR SNYDER
THOR HAGEN

GIRLS' MATCH — DOT DOTSON vs. JUDY GLOV__
2 OTHER GREAT BOUTS

Watch the Great Stars of Wrestling Every Saturday Night on __
Channel 11, from the Khorassan Room of Hotel Chase.
JOE GARAGIOLA, Announcer

ROCK HUNTER

Feb. 19 1978
Via Check # 4346 — #1500.00   March 5, 1978
                                      Via Check # 4388 — #1500.00
Ric Flair
Dick Murdoch ———————— 307 —   Mickey Doragula —————— 40 —
Pat O'Connor ———————— 238 —   Chas Verleter ———————— 50 —
Evan Johnson ———————— 192 —   Joe Tangaro —————————— 52 —
David Von Erich —————— 100 —   Bennie Romeug ———————— 70 —
Ted DiBiase ————————— 100 —   David Nevans —————————— 70 —
Scott Casey ————————— 138 —   Karl Offles ——————————— 70 —
Bennie Romeug ———————— 75 —   Buzz Tyler —————————————— 70 —
Alexis Smirnoff ————————— 75 — David Von Erich ————————— 70 —
Steve Cooper ——————————— 75 —   Sehu ———————————————————— 70 —
Mike Pappas ———————————— 70 —   Steve Howe ————————————— 75 —
Max Blue ——————————————— 70 —   Scott Casey ———————————— 75 —
Mark Scioro ———————————— 70 —   Buck Robley —————————————— 75 —
Joe Tangaro ———————————— 52 —   Kevin Sullivan ———————————— 75 —
Eddie Smith ———————————— 52 —   John Valiant ——————————————— 90 —
Mickey Doragula ——————— 40 —   Pat O'Connor ———————————— 193 —
                        1720   Terry Funk ——————————————— 310 —
                                                            1553

Check # 4346 ——————— $1500.00
Check # 4367 ——————— 200.00   Check # 4388 — $1500.00
                     #1720.00   Check # 4403 — 53.00
                                              1553.00

JOHNNY VALENTINE: This tall, tan, bleached-blonde hunk had everything he needed to be one of the best-ever baby faces. Instead, Valentine used his great looks and skill to become one of the best of the bad guys from the late 1940s, through the 1950s, and into the 1960s. When he tangled with other ruffians, though, Valentine became a tremendous fan favorite, particularly in the mid-1960s and into the 1970s as he alternated between being a villainous heel and a baby-face hero. Few wrestlers could connect on an emotional level with fans like Valentine could, no matter if you loved him or hated him. Fans flocked to see him wrestle, and they were always treated to a splendid match that included more than just powerful post-match comments. Johnny started his nearly three-decade career in 1947, and he quickly became a fan favorite thanks to nationwide TV when wrestling was an early smash hit in the 1950s. Johnny could also stir things up when he pounded rivals like Pat O'Connor, Cowboy Bob Ellis, and John Paul Henning in the early days of *Wrestling at the Chase*. Battles with the likes of those greats as well as Lou Thesz, Bruno Sammartino, Buddy Rogers, Antonino Rocca, Harley Race,

Bobo Brazil, and Jack Brisco all over the world made him a superstar. Valentine was an amazing drawing card not only in St. Louis but everywhere he appeared. Thesz always pointed to Valentine as one of the select opponents that he truly respected, because Johnny was so tough and durable. His career was cut short in 1975 after an airplane accident with Ric Flair and promoter David Crockett in North Carolina. Valentine was partially paralyzed. His son, Greg, had a productive career and also earned main events in St. Louis. But Greg had big shoes to fill, because Johnny Valentine was one of wrestling's true superstars. Johnny Valentine's later years were filled with many medical issues before he passed away peacefully on April 24, 2001, at the age of 72.

Johnny Valentine and Cowboy Bob Ellis

Johnny
Valentine
COURTESY OF
GETTY IMAGES

Johnny Valentine works Bulldog Brower outside the ring amidst a little tossed popcorn.

109

Whipper Watson under Gene Kiniski's boot outside the ring as the referee turns his head

110

GENE KINISKI was known as "Big Thunder," and when he was at his best in the 1960s, he was an NWA champion and a top draw all over the world. He was a headliner from the 1950s all the way until 1982, when he battled Ric Flair in St. Louis. Kiniski, an Edmonton native, held the NWA title from 1966 to 1969. A large man with quick, athletic moves and relentless energy, he ruled the ring with relative ease. After a brief pro football career in Canada with the Edmonton Eskimos, Kiniski started wrestling in 1953. He gained quick fame with partner John Tolos as they won the international tag-team crown in 1954. Kiniski took on NWA legend and champ Lou Thesz for the first time the same year. He switched partners, teaming up with Lord Blears, and the duo won the San Francisco version of the world tag-team crown three times. In 1956, he took the Texas crown, wrestling as Gene Kelly. His longtime feud with Whipper Billy Watson began in 1957 when he partnered with Buddy Rogers against Watson and Pat O'Connor. The rivalry gained a national audience as they battled in main events all over Canada. Gene tried in vain to get the NWA title from champions such as Watson, Thesz, and Dick Hutton through 1957. Kiniski moved in 1960 to Minneapolis and beat Verne Gagne for the AWA title in 1961. He was an early star on *Wrestling at the Chase* in St. Louis, thanks to his in-ring feud with Cowboy Bob Ellis and a running verbal duel with announcer Joe Garagiola. Battles against Rogers, his matches with Thesz, and a tour in Japan in 1964 gained Kiniski more attention and praise. His star continued to rise when he clashed with Bruno Sammartino, a.k.a. the Italian Strongman, in 1964 and 1965 on the East Coast. Kiniski's hard work and dedication finally resulted in his winning the NWA prize in 1966, when he beat

Cowboy Bob Ellis

Gene Kiniski
COURTESY OF
WIKIMEDIA COMMONS

Bruno Sammartino
COURTESY OF
WIKIMEDIA COMMONS

Thesz in St. Louis. Kiniski didn't shy away from anybody for the next three years before he was dethroned by Dory Funk Jr. in 1969. Gene actually lived in St. Louis during the time he held the championship. He later won the Missouri title in 1973 and was a top challenger for the NWA championships while he was also promoting in Vancouver. Few in history competed as long and as hard as "Big Thunder." On April 14, 2010, at the age of 81, Gene passed away due to complications from cancer.

PENNY BANNER: Women wrestlers had been around since the early days of the sport, and local girl Penny Banner became a fan favorite. Mary Ann Kostecki was born and raised in St. Louis. She was discovered by promoter Sam Muchnick in 1954 while she was working as a cocktail waitress. She won a bet with Muchnick that she could do 200 sit-ups. That victory set in motion a chain of events that led her to Columbus, Ohio, to train with promoter Billy Wolfe. Along with the training came a name change to Penny Banner. Athletic and beautiful, Banner was an instant hit as she became one of the top female wrestlers of all time. She also became known as a dirty wrestler and was always tagged as the bad guy in her matches. She held both the Canadian and USA Ladies Tag Team Championships on three different occasions (1956, 1957, and 1958–1959) and the Ladies Texas Championship. However, perhaps her greatest feat was becoming the first American Wrestling Alliance champion in August 1961. Looking back on her career, Penny was quoted in a 1961 article in *Big Time Wrestling* saying that being a woman wrestler is much better than a college education: "I get to see so many places in this world, places most people just read about." Banner retired in 1977 and passed away in 2008 at the age of 73.

Penny Banner
COURTESY OF NICK REDNOUR

COMICS COURTESY OF NICK REDNOUR

In addition to Penny Banner, there were a few other key women who climbed into the St. Louis wrestling rings including that of *Wrestling at the Chase*. Debbie Combs followed in her mother Cora's wrestling footsteps and had a Hall of Fame career beginning in the early 1980s. Another women wrestler who caught St. Louis's and the nation's attention during the golden years of the sport was the Fabulous Moolah, who would win her first championship in 1956 and continue her reign off and on for the next 28 years.

The Fabulous Moolah
COURTESY OF GETTY IMAGES

Debbie Combs

Debbie Combs (*right*) and her mother, Cora

THE FUNKS: When ranking the greatest wrestling families in the sport of professional wrestling, the Funks are near the top of the list. Based out of the Double Cross Ranch in Amarillo, Texas, patriarch Dory Funk Sr. and his two sons regularly crawled into the wrestling ring in St. Louis and were a favorite at the Chase. Both sons, Dory Jr. and Terry, became world heavyweight champions. Dory Jr., a tactician in the ring who would punish his opponents to submission with his famous toeholds, began competing in 1963. He won his first NWA World Championship in 1969 and held it through 1973. With ever-aggressive brother Terry making his debut in 1965 and capturing the NWA World Championship 10 years later, the Funks became the only brothers to have held the prestigious honor. When they were not pursuing solo matches, the two brothers formed one of the most successful tag teams of the 1970s.

The Funk Family—Terry, Dory Sr., and Dory Jr.

Dory Funk Jr. and Johnny Valentine

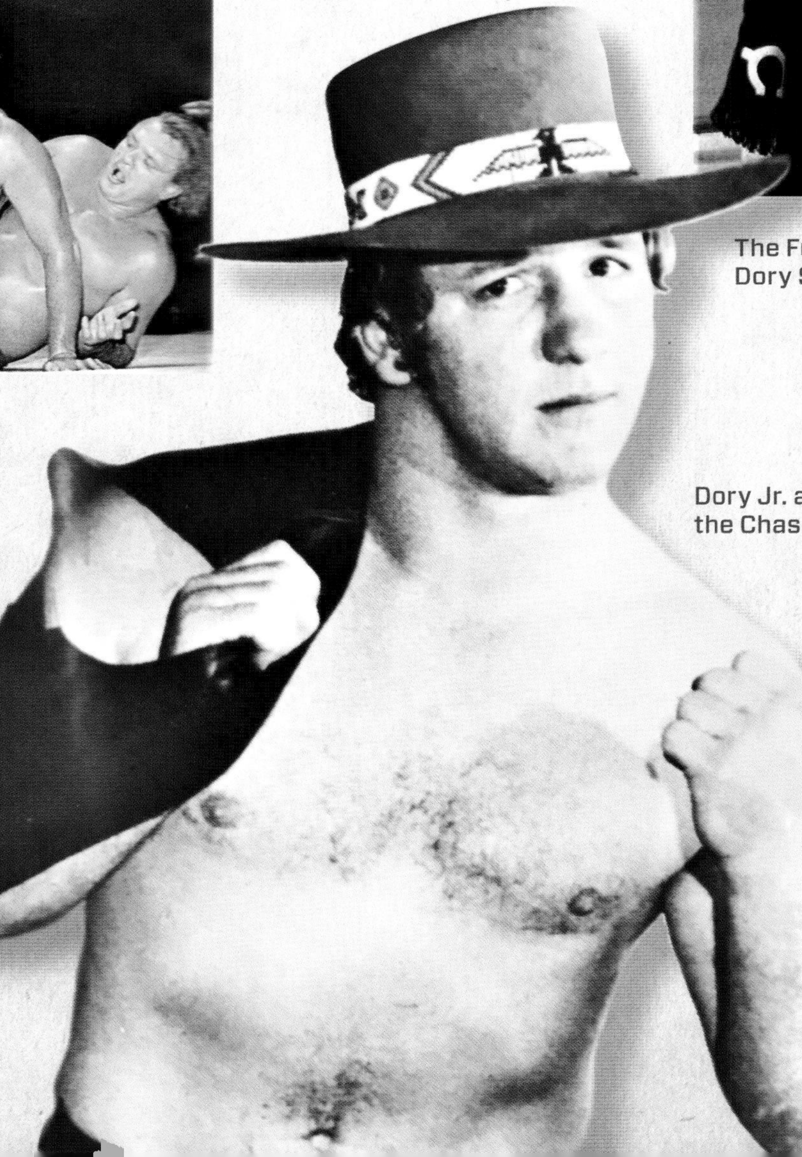

Dory Jr. and George Abel at the Chase, December 1969

Terry Funk

BARON VON RASCHKE: After a stint in the military and then in teaching, Raschke found his way into the ring and eventually added the title "Baron Von" as his given name. Although he grew up as a star football player and wrestler in Nebraska, the German military slant became his adopted wrestling persona. With a Prussian goose step, Von Raschke would march toward an opponent with the military-like assignment that "I am ordered to win! I must win! And I will win!" Then the Baron would finish his foe with his dominating "brain claw." During the 1970s and 1980s, Von Raschke became a top box-office draw, winning many individual titles, and he also partnered with Maurice "Mad Dog" Vachon to win the world tag-team championship.

Baron Von Raschke taking on Pat O'Connor at the Chase in April 1969

Baron Von Raschke's brain claw

The Baron applies the brain claw for a win!

Baron Von Raschke

Jack Brisco and
Terry Funk

THE BRISCO BROTHERS from Oklahoma formed another great family combination. Older brother Jack was a two-time world champion in the NWA and a multi-time NWA tag-team champion with his younger brother Jerry. Jack is recognized as one of the top professional wrestlers of the 1970s, and both were regulars in St. Louis. Jack, in fact, was a star college wrestler at Oklahoma State, winning a national championship title in 1965 after finishing the year before as runner-up. In doing so, he became the first Native American to win an NCAA wrestling national championship. He would win his first professional world championship title in 1973 when he defeated Harley Race. He held that title for over 500 days, one of the longest runs in professional wrestling. Jack lost the title in December 1974 to Giant Baba but promptly won it back four days later and would hold on to the title until he was defeated by Terry Funk the following December. Jack continued to wrestle until 1985 and passed away following complications from open heart surgery in 2010 at the age of 68.

Brother Jerry, who was five years younger than Jack, won numerous singles championships throughout the 1970s before winning the NWA World Junior Heavyweight Championship in 1981. He and his brother would hold the NWA National Tag Team Championship for the last time in 1983, and both would later work behind the scenes in professional wrestling. They would also get to see one of their biggest discoveries break through as well. Through their training, the Briscos had come across a young wrestling wannabe who happened to be playing bass in a rock band called Ruckus. That guitar player was named Terry Bollea. The Brisco brothers made the necessary contacts for him and set him on his way to become the legendary Hulk Hogan.

Jack Brisco

Jerry Brisco
COURTESY OF WIKIMEDIA COMMONS

The Von Erich family

Kevin
David
Fritz
Kerry
Von Erich

THE VON ERICHS: When looking through the family histories of professional wrestling, the Von Erichs were probably the first big-name family dynasty of professional wrestling. The family was a regular part of the St. Louis scene beginning with the patriarch, Fritz, who like Von Raschke took on a villainous German identity as one of wrestling's toughest heels. Fritz wasn't German. He was a Texan named Jack Adkisson who tried his hand like so many others at professional football but couldn't make the cut. He found success and a new moniker in professional wrestling, where he became a multi-time world champion. Known for his "Iron Claw" hold, Fritz was a regular stud in Sam Muchnick's wrestling stable in the 1960s. Von Erich had great success in St. Louis working for Sam and the NWA. He was always considered a top contender for the world heavyweight championship and battled all the big-name stars. After Von Erich

lost the championship in 1967 to Gene Kiniski in St. Louis, Muchnick helped him become the promoter of the Texas region, which included Dallas, Houston, and San Antonio. There, Von Erich enjoyed much success with his wrestlers and television promotions.

His personal life had its trials and tribulations. Sons Kevin, David, and Kerry Von Erich worked with their father and turned the group into the hottest thing going at the time. Fritz tutored his sons and even teamed with them in tag matches. As a result, the Von Erich boys were a hit with fans in St. Louis and all over the country, in no small part because of Fritz's reputation and skill. Five of the six sons preceded their father in death, two by accident and three by suicide. Today, only Kevin is still alive, carrying on the legacy of the Von Erichs in retirement.

David and Fritz Von Erich

Kevin Von Erich

JOE TANGARO was a Utah native who like many other wrestlers was on his way to an NFL career after starring in both football and wrestling at the University of Utah. After serving in the navy during World War II, Tangaro went with professional wrestling after meeting Sam Muchnick and realizing that grappling paid better than football at the time. Joe wrestled solo but also had a lucrative tag-team career in tandem with his Utah football teammate Guy Brunetti. In fact, for years the two wrestled under the name the Brunetti Brothers, with Joe using the moniker Joe Brunetti. Together they took the Canadian and US tag-team titles and a host of other regional ones as well. The good-looking Italian grappler soon became a regular in Muchnick's circuit and regularly appeared on *Wrestling at the Chase*.

Even with all the success he had in the ring, Joe always wanted a career that was in line with his Italian heritage and his love of family and food. By the mid-1960s, he began limiting his wrestling engagements to be at home with his family and to pursue his passion for cooking. Using the many recipes he had picked up touring the country during his wrestling career, he became more than a St. Louis fixture inside the ring; he became a St. Louis restaurateur as well. Joe Tangaro's Chariton Restaurant on South Broadway, just south of downtown

AFTER THE . . .
Wrestling Matches
. . . visit . . .
WARREN BOCKWINKEL'S
RESTAURANT and BAR
113 NORTH BROADWAY

★

- CHICKEN
- STEAKS
  - CHOPS
    - SANDWICHES
       OF ALL KINDS

BUDWEISER ON TAP

MEET
YOUR FAVORITE WRESTLER HERE!

Sincerely,
Warren Bockwinkel

St. Louis, became a culinary fixture for 20 years, before he retired and sold it in 1984. In his later years, Joe suffered from Lou Gehrig's disease before passing away in 1997 at the age of 70. There were many wrestlers who grew up in the area or starred in the professional wrestling capital of the 1950s and 1960s.

Like Joe Tangaro, the Bockwinkel family made a mark in the ring as well as in St. Louis's culinary arena. St. Louis–reared Warren Bockwinkel competed in the early days of the NWA and gained fame as one of the first grapplers to appear on the small screen as professional wrestling took to the airwaves. Besides training his son Nick, who would go on to star in the AWA and win their heavyweight championship six times during the 1970s and 1980s, Warren operated Warren Bockwinkel's Restaurant and Bar in downtown St. Louis, which became known for years as the place to visit after wrestling matches.

Joe Tangaro

Warren Bockwinkel

Harley Race, the Fabulous Moolah, and Nick Bockwinkel

The house the SICW fans built

SOUTHERN ILLINOIS
SICW
CHAMPIONSHIP WRESTLING

PART 5

TODAY, TOMORROW, AND THE FUTURE

St. Louis Wrestling
Hall of Fame Alumni

Wild Bill Longson	Penny Banner
Larry Matysik	Jack Brisco
Sam Muchnick	King Kong Brody
Pat O'Connor	Dick the Bruiser
Harley Race	Ric Flair
Buddy Rogers	Dory Funk, Jr.
Joe Schoenberger	Joe Garagiola
Lou Thesz	Mickey Garagiola
Johnny Valentine	Bobby Heenan
Fritz Von Erich	Rocky Johnson
Kevin Von Erich	Gene Kiniski
David Von Erich	Terry Funk
Kerry Von Erich	Dick Murdoch
Baron Von Raschke	Ted Dibiase
Lee Warren	Wilber Snyder
Cowboy Bob Ellis	Rip Hawk
Bill Apter	John Paul Henning
Joe Tangaro	Big Bill Miller
Ken Patera	Charles Venator
Ed Smith	Edouard Carpentier
Bob Backlund	Whipper Billy Watson
Bob Orton Sr.	Debbie Combs

PROFESSIONAL WRESTLING IN ST. LOUIS TODAY

IT'S BEEN ALMOST 40 YEARS since the ringside bell was last rung on *Wrestling at the Chase*. In the ensuing years, there were a few locally produced televised wrestling programs that tried to follow its success, but they didn't last. It's not because professional wrestling doesn't exist any longer in St. Louis or that fans aren't interested. The fact is that St. Louisans still regularly turn out at events in large numbers. They watch WWE televised matches throughout the week on cable television networks, and several times a year they fill the stands in local arenas when the WWE's professional tour comes to town. But more importantly, they regularly fill the halls of the South Broadway Athletic Club's Mid-Missouri Wrestling Alliance events or head just across the Mississippi River to the Southern Illinois Championship Wrestling Club. Both clubs continue to hold live matches on a regular basis before sold-out crowds.

Southern Illinois Championship Wrestling (SICW), headquartered in St. Clair County, Illinois, was formed in 1975 by Herb Simmons. Over 40 years later, they still offer a steady calendar of events throughout southern Illinois and Missouri in the tradition of matches held at *Wrestling at the Chase*. Their ties to the iconic program come directly from its founder and promoter, Herb Simmons, and his longtime partner and the voice of *Wrestling at the Chase*, Larry Matysik. In recent times, a viewer flipping through cable channels may have gotten confused if they happened to stop on a televised SICW wrestling program and thought they were once again watching *Wrestling at the Chase*. That was because Larry was back at the microphone delivering details of the matches. He, in fact, provided play-by-play for over 500 SICW events. In over four decades of matches, SICW has brought into the ring many of the greatest grapplers from the golden years of professional wrestling. Former star wrestlers like Dory Funk, the Briscos, Baron Von Raschke,

In 1959, the fans started coming to *Wrestling at the Chase*, and today they continue to fill the seats at SICW.

Crusher Blackwell, Bruiser Brody, and Lou Thesz have appeared at their events as well as in the ring. Not only do their shows provide outstanding entertainment and memories of wrestling heroes, their generosity in promoting and hosting these events helps raise funds for local organizations, first responders, and many other groups. (For more information, visit their website at sicw.org.)

Wrestling greats are always around at SICW. Here Ken Patera, Rocky Johnson, Grizzlies baseball team owner Rich Sauget, Larry Matysik, Baron Von Raschke, and Jerry "The King" Lawler participate in a SICW benefit at the Grizzlies' stadium.

While the South Broadway Athletic Club (SBAC) has been in existence for over 110 years, it has been home to the Mid-Missouri Wrestling Alliance (MMWA) since 1985. The MMWA is an American independent professional wrestling promotion. It has had a close relationship over the years with SICW, but each organization has evolved its own different style and dynamic. The SICW programs under Herb Simmons continue to focus on what people have referred to as "old school," or simply put, the style of professional wrestling's golden years. In contrast, the matches at the SBAC, led over the years by the late Tony Casta, tend to be more modern in the genre of wrestling seen in WWE promotions and matches. Their events are held once a month with a few others sporadically held in nearby St. Louis arenas. Until 2014, the MMWA had a local 30-minute television program titled *The Wild World of Wrestling*, which aired on Friday nights across local cable television affiliates. For more information, visit their website at prowrestling.fandom.com/wiki/mid-missouri_wrestling_alliance.

While locally produced professional wrestling no longer fills the airwaves of mid-America, those memories of wrestlers climbing into the ring at the Chase Park Plaza's Khorassan Room retain a special place in the hearts and minds of so many people across the region.

Herb Simmons from SICW and Tony Casta from the SBAC were inducted together into the St. Louis Independent Wrestling Hall of Fame.

A capacity crowd at South Broadway watches Ricky Cruz battle Curtis Wylde.

May those special Saturday night remembrances remain fresh for all who watched either in person or on television all those years ago! To those cheering ringside at SICW or SBAC matches today, it is hoped that they take the time to think about the men and women who got dressed to the nines and sat at tables with red and white checkered tablecloths in one of the poshest venues in town to watch men and women toil in physical combat. Finally, it is hoped that this book will help us remember the time when St. Louis was the center of the professional wrestling universe and *Wrestling at the Chase* was its biggest ticket.

FROM SAM TO LARRY TO HERB— A TRIBUTE TO THE MAN WHO CONTINUES THE TRADITION TODAY

Wednesday night
Wrestling at the Chase

HERB SIMMONS HAS BEEN a lifelong fan of professional wrestling. Through the Southern Illinois Championship Wrestling club, he remains focused on preserving the old-school tradition of professional wrestling that brought viewers to the Chase Hotel and television sets weekly. In his own words, Herb highlights the importance of professional wrestling and its memories:

"Professional wrestling was the action-packed sport I grew up enjoying, no, grew up loving. As a young boy growing up in the housing projects in East St. Louis, Illinois, I became hooked on professional wrestling. Being one of five children raised in a single-parent home, my mother had to be mom and dad. One of the things she and I had in common was wrestling. We loved turning on the twelve-inch black-and-white television on Wednesday nights listening to Joe Garagiola welcome us to another week of *Wrestling at the Chase*. 'Wall to wall, tree top tall' was the one salutation that I still remember Joe using quite often as he would lead into the lineup of that night's action. I knew early in life that professional wrestling was what I enjoyed more than any other sport. Yes, I said sport, because back then that's what many of us believed.

Growing up, I continued to follow all the greats who appeared on Wrestling at the Chase, at the Kiel Auditorium, and the St. Louis Arena/Checkerdome. Dick the Bruiser, Cowboy Bob Ellis, Fritz Von Erich, Johnny Valentine, the Briscos, the Funks, Harley Race, and Bruiser Brody (we didn't call him "King Kong") were just some of the greats. Can't forget Lou

Thesz, Pat O'Connor, Sam Muchnick, or my dear friend Larry Matysik. The amazing part of my life was growing up admiring all these individuals, the greats of the business, and then later getting to work with all of them. It was a dream come true for a young man growing up.

Larry Matysik, Sam Muchnick, and Herb Simmons

Herb and Bruiser Brody

for 34 years and working my adult life in public safety, I've always enjoyed and loved professional wrestling. I've been blessed with the ownership of the records from *Wrestling at the Chase*, along with footage from the television programs and the collection of the programs listing the matches over the years of its existence. I will always be grateful to Sam Muchnick and my dear friend Larry Matysik for having confidence and trust in me and for introducing me to all the greats of *Wrestling at the Chase*."

Super fan Darla Staggs, Larry, and Herb

Herb in the middle between Bruiser Bob Sweetan (*left*) and Spike Huber

I soon got to meet Sam Muchnick through Larry, and the most important thing Sam taught me was to keep my ears open and my mouth shut. He said, 'If I followed that advice like he taught Larry, that I would go a long way in the business of professional wrestling.' He was right. February of 2021 was my 47th year in the business. Some have stated I'm the longest-running promoter in the country and the last connection to the St. Louis office that was operated by Sam for all those years. Even with being the mayor of my community

A FINAL CHAPTER

ACROSS AMERICAN SOCIETY since World War II, professional wrestling has had a dramatic impact on millions of people's lives in so many ways. Beyond the kayfabe, people believed or perhaps just wanted to believe and came out better for it. Programs like *Wrestling at the Chase* set individuals' weekly schedules with matches that became battles of good versus evil. In the end, those from the dark side generally got their due, and when the show was over people could go home or turn off their television sets with smiles on their faces. Everyone was happy, and they couldn't wait to be back next week.

It's now been nearly four decades since *Wrestling at the Chase* went off the air. I hope this book will keep its legacy alive by bringing back personal memories of those who watched each week or passed the tales of the glory days of old-time wrestling to new generations. As many of these warriors within the ring have passed on, let us look back, remember, and smile, because the memories of that time and that show have not left us.

Wrestling legends one more time!

Lou Thesz, Jack Brisco, Gene Kiniski, Harley Race, Dory Funk Jr., Sam Muchnick, Terry Funk
COURTESY OF IRENE MUELLER

Crusher Blackwell and
King Kong Brody

PART! 6

APPENDIX

Black Jack Mulligan, Bobby Heenan, Black Jack Lanza, and Dusty Rhodes

Mickey Garagiola

FACTS AND MYTHS OF WRESTLING AT THE CHASE

TEST YOUR KNOWLEDGE of *Wrestling at the Chase* by guessing which of the following are facts and which are myths.

1. Andre the Giant once wrestled on the program.
2. A Super Bowl champion football player wrestled on the program.
3. Dwayne "The Rock" Johnson wrestled on the program.
4. A famous governor wrestled on the program.
5. Kamala used his Ugandan homeland rituals of marching to the ring wearing an African mask while carrying a spear and shield to intimidate his opponents and then wrestled in bare feet wearing war paint and a loincloth.
6. Hulk Hogan, a crowd favorite of the mid-1980s and into the 1990s, climbed into the ring at the Chase.
7. He was a tough guy in the ring as well as on the stage. Lou Thesz performed in *Guys and Dolls* at St. Louis's Muny Opera in Forest Park.

Kamala the Ugandan Giant

Andre the Giant taking on Bruiser Bob Sweetan
COURTESY OF WIKIMEDIA COMMONS

THE ANSWERS

1. Myth. Andre the Giant, the 7-foot 4-inch, 529-pound mauler was a star in the ring and in film. He starred in the box office hit *The Princess Bride* and appeared in St. Louis many times, but he never wrestled on *Wrestling at the Chase*. He did, however, crawl into the ring at Kiel and the Checkerdome.

2. Myth. Intimidating 6-foot 9-inch Ernie "The Cat" Ladd did step into the ring at *Wrestling at the Chase*. However, he never made it to the Super Bowl as a football player. Ernie Ladd was one of the largest men in the NFL at the time as a star defensive tackle for the Kansas City Chiefs during the 1967 and 1968 seasons. The problem was that "The Cat" played for the team that was sandwiched between the Chiefs' two Super Bowl appearances following the 1966 and 1969 seasons.

3. Myth. Dwayne "The Rock" Johnson never appeared on *Wrestling at the Chase*. However, his father, Rocky Johnson, a holder of many wrestling titles, was a regular in St. Louis and appeared on the program multiple times during its run. Not only did Rocky wrestle, he was a regular sparring partner of George Foreman and Muhammad Ali.

4. Fact. Future Minnesota governor Jessie "The Body" Ventura went inside the ropes on *Wrestling at the Chase* in the latter years of the program.

5. Myth. While Kamala used Ugandan rituals of marching to the ring wearing an African mask and carrying a spear and shield to intimidate his opponents—and he even wrestled in bare feet wearing war paint and a loincloth—he wasn't from the African continent. He was born and raised just down the river from St. Louis in Senatobia, Mississippi.

Ernie "The Cat" Ladd (*left*) and Bobo Brazil

Hulk Hogan
COURTESY OF
WIKIMEDIA COMMONS

6. Fact—sort of! Hulk Hogan, a crowd favorite of the mid-1980s into the 1990s and also a star wrestler in Sylvester Stallone's third installment of the *Rocky* film series as Thunderlips, actually did climb into the ring and wrestle at the Chase. However, he never wrestled during the program's tenure from 1959 to 1983. But he did wrestle at the Chase in 1984 in episodes produced and filmed by the WWF.

7. Fact. The former world champion performed in a week's run of *Guys and Dolls* at the famed Muny Opera in August 1969 along with Barbara McNair, Jane Kean, Bill Elliott, and Soupy Sales.

Rocky Johnson

137

DO YOU REMEMBER THESE FAMOUS HOLDS AND MOVES?

Verne Gagne's Chart of Basic Submission and Pinning Holds

Pictures posed by Verne Gagne (former Big-10, NCAA and Olympic mat star, and leading heavyweight challenger) and Don Beitelman

Stag BEER

Watch Wrestling on Television Sponsored by STAG Beer

ST. LOUIS: KSD-TV   MEMPHIS: WMCT

COURTESY OF
CODY KNIPPING

EACH ESTABLISHED PROFESSIONAL WRESTLER had his or her own branded hold and/or finishing move incorporated into their routines. Here is a summary of some of the more prominent maneuvers performed by *Wrestling at the Chase* grapplers:

BOBO BRAZIL, one of the first successful African American wrestlers, used his head to win matches with his "Coco Butt" maneuver. By banging the front of his head against his opponent, Bobo would knock them down prior to pinning them.

COWBOY BOB ELLIS created the "Bulldog Headlock" based on how he would capture steers during his days in the rodeo. Ellis would grab an opponent's head and jump forward, so that Ellis would land, often in a sitting position, and drive his opponent's face into the mat.

Houston Harris,
a.k.a. Bobo Brazil
COURTESY OF
GETTY IMAGES

139

King Kong/Bruiser Brody would finish off his opponents with the "Flying Knee Drop" to the upper chest before pinning them.

Dick the Bruiser would finish with the "Atomic Drop" by getting behind an opponent and then putting his head under the rival's shoulder. The Bruiser would then lift his opponent up, and drop him tailbone-first on to his knee. Initially the Bruiser's Atomic Drop involved him jumping off the top rope of the ring and landing a foot into his opponent's chest. That was soon outlawed due to use of the ring ropes.

Ric Flair further popularized the "Figure-Four Leg Lock" as his finishing move of choice.

Dory Funk Jr. used the "Spinning Toehold" to finish a victorious match. Rip Hawk used the "Reverse Neckbreaker."

John Paul Henning is remembered for developing the submissive "Bow and Arrow" hold. Henning would grab his opponent's chin and leg and while placing both of his feet in the middle of the man's back and pulling at the same time. In execution, Henning became the arrow and his opponent the bow.

Cowboy Bob Orton Jr. was famous for using the piledriver and suplex off the top rope.

Gene Kiniski used the "Backbreaker" to win his championship title match with Lou Thesz.

Pat O'Connor used the "Reverse Rolling Cradle" to pin his opponent by holding his shoulders to the mat for a three count. O'Connor was also known for using his leg split to weaken his opponent.

Brody delivering the Flying Knee Drop

Cowboy Bob Orton Jr.

Funk putting his finishing move on "Big Thunder" Gene Kiniski in 1968

Funk's toehold move

140

Pat O'Connor with the leg split on Lord Alfred Hayes

Buddy Rogers first created the "Figure-Four Leg Lock," in which the wrestler stands over his opponent, who is lying down on the mat face up, and then grabs his opponent's leg. The wrestler does a spinning toehold and grabs the other leg, crossing them into a "4" shape (thus the name), then falls to the mat and puts pressure on the opponent's crossed legs with his own.

Lou Thesz created the "Lou Thesz Press" by jumping toward a standing opponent and knocking him onto his back with Thesz then sitting on the opponent's chest and pinning him in a body scissors.

Johnny Valentine used his elbow to the back of the neck and head of his opponent with his "Brain Buster" move to knock him to the mat, which then allowed him to win the match with a pin.

Wilbur Snyder was known for his powerful hammerlock.

And then there was always the very simple kneeing of an opponent as shown by Bruno Sammartino.

Bob Geigel's signature move was the "Boston Crab."

Baron Von Raschke used the "Brain Claw" to finish off opponents by clutching his large hand across the head of his opponent and applying pressure until he submitted. Fritz Von Erich had a similar moved called the "Iron Claw."

Von Raschke's brain claw

Bruno Sammartino knees his opponent.
COURTESY OF GETTY IMAGES

Wilbur Snyder (*right*) twists champion Lou Thesz with a powerful hammerlock.

THE BIGGEST FEUDS OF *WRESTLING AT THE CHASE*

- Jack Brisco and all members of the Funk family
- Harley Race and Dusty Rhodes
- Ted DiBiase and all the Funks
- Abdullah the Butcher and Jack Brisco
- Dick the Bruiser and Black Jack Lanza
- Johnny Valentine and Pat O'Connor
- Gene Kiniski and Cowboy Bob Ellis
- Whipper Billy Watson and Gene Kiniski
- King Kong Brody and Kamala the Ugandan Giant
- Abdullah the Butcher and King Kong Brody
- Big John Studd and Ted DiBiase

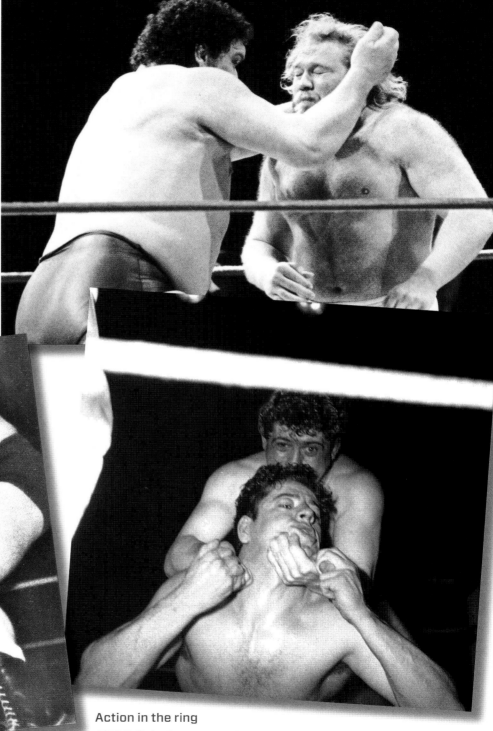

Andre the Giant fights Big John Studd.
COURTESY OF GETTY IMAGES

Gene Kiniski working Pat O'Connor

Action in the ring
COURTESY OF GETTY IMAGES

PROFESSIONAL WRESTLING IN ST. LOUIS

SEPTEMBER 1922
The Chase Hotel opens in St. Louis.

APRIL 1941
Sam Muchnick breaks ties with Tom Packs.

JULY 1948
A group of promoters formalizes the National Wrestling Alliance in Waterloo, Iowa.

1950
Sam Muchnick becomes president of the National Wrestling Alliance, a position he retains for 22 years.

MAY 3, 1953
Wrestling from the St. Louis House premieres on KSDK-TV.

APRIL 1955
Wrestling from the St. Louis House is canceled. Locally produced televised wrestling ceases.

MARCH 1942
Sam Muchnick promotes his first program.

SEPTEMBER 1949 .... **MARCH 1955**
Wrestling from Marigold is televised in St. Louis on KSDK-TV and WTVI.

JUNE 1932
Sam Muchnick leaves the *St. Louis Star* for a position with Tom Packs's promotions.

FEBRUARY 1949
Sam Muchnick–promoted wrestling program has its first sellout at St. Louis's Kiel Auditorium.

1958
The St. Louis Wrestling Club is formed.

Sam Muchnick and Harold Koplar sit next to each other on an airplane ride and discuss a televised wrestling program for St. Louis .

TODAY—PROFESSIONAL WRESTLING still generates a large turnout for WWE and locally promoted events across the St. Louis region. It also captures a large following on television networks across local airwaves. Even with this following, it is the memories of *Wrestling at the Chase* that remain the pinnacle memory of professional wrestling for generations of fans growing up in Middle America.

TIMELINE

1959
Television station
KPLR-TV premieres.

Wrestling at the Chase
premieres on KPLR-TV from
the Khorassan Room of the
Chase Hotel featuring Jim
LaRock vs. the Mighty Atlas,
Rip Hawk vs. Ray Spindola,
and Whipper Billy Watson
vs. Bob Orton.

JANUARY 1982
Muchnick promotes
his last card before a
sellout crowd at the
Checkerdome and
retires.

Muchnick sells the
St. Louis Wrestling Club
to the triumvirate of
Verne Gagne, Bob Geigel,
and Pat O'Connor with
Harley Race soon joining
the partnership.

SEPTEMBER 1983
KPLR-TV ends its
relationship with the
St. Louis Wrestling
Club and establishes a
new relationship with
Vince McMahon's WWF
promotions.

OCTOBER 1983
Larry Matysik's St. Louis
Wrestling Enterprises
production's last show at
the Checkerdome

FEBRUARY 1984
KPLR-TV and the WWF
move their televised
matches from the Chase
to Kiel Auditorium.

SEPTEMBER 1984
KPLR-TV and the WWF
hold one final taping of
professional wrestling in
the Khorassan Room of
the Chase Park Plaza.

DECEMBER 1998
Sam Muchnick passes
away.

AUGUST 2010
Mickey Garagiola passes
away.

NOVEMBER 1967
Wrestling at the Chase
moves from the
Khorassan Room to the
KPLR-TV studio.

JUNE 1983
Larry Matysik promotes
his first show at the
Checkerdome under
his St. Louis Wrestling
Enterprises company.

AUGUST 1983
Larry Matysik's televised
wrestling promotion
show appears on
KDNL-TV 30.

DECEMBER 1983
KPLR-TV in conjunction
with the WWF once
again televises wrestling
from the Chase Hotel's
Khorassan Room and
introduces new names to
the local wrestling scene
including the first WWF
matches of Gene Okerlund
and Hulk Hogan.

JIM CROCKETT
PROMOTIONS

1985
The St. Louis
Wrestling Club
is purchased
by Jim Crockett
Promotions and
is absorbed into
what becomes Ted
Turner's World
Championship
Wrestling, which are
all now defunct.

NOVEMBER 2018
Larry Matysik passes
away.

MAY 2017
Billy Crogan
purchases NWA.

SAM MUCHNICK'S MOST MEMORABLE WRESTLING CARDS

IN MEMORY OF SAM MUCHNICK on his passing on December 30, 1998, at age 93, *St. Louis Post-Dispatch* writer Keith Schildroth provided a summary of Sam's most memorable wrestling cards.[22]

- **Lou Thesz vs. Whipper Billy Watson** at Kiel in the mid-1950s for the world title.
- **Thesz vs. Killer Kowalski** at Kiel in the late 50s pitted a wrestler (Thesz) against a brawler (Kowalski).
- **Buddy Rogers vs. Johnny Valentine** at Kiel in 1961.
- **Gene Kiniski vs. Cowboy Bob Ellis**, the first big feud on Wrestling at the Chase in the early 60s.
- **Lou Thesz vs. Pat O'Connor** at Kiel in the late 60s. An actual one-hour wrestling match.
- **Dick the Bruiser vs. Kiniski** at Kiel in a Texas Death Match in 1965.
- **Thesz vs. Kiniski** at Kiel on January 7, 1966. Thesz lost the title here to the number 1 villain.

DICK "THE BRUISER"   .250   Reno, Nevada

9/19/69 - with Lanza in no.dec. against
          Dory Sr. and Terry Funk
10/17/69 - winning side with Raschke, Waldo vs.
          O'Connor, Ladd, Watson
11/7/69 - beat Black Jack Lanza on C.O.R.
11/21/69 - with Wilbur Snyder, beat Lanza and
          Raschke; won 1st fall over Raschke and 3rd
          fall via disqualification
12/5/69 - won Texas death match from
          Black Jack Lanza
1/9/70 - lost to Dory Funk, Jr. via disq.
          FINED AND INDEFINITELY SUSPENDED

JACK BRISCO (5)
     236   Blackwell, Okla.

4/19/74 - beat Dory Funk Jr., Brisco won only
          fall achieved within hour limit
6/14/74 - one hour draw with Dory Funk Jr.,
          each man won one fall within limit
10/4/74 - beat Johnny Valentine 2/3 falls
11/15/74 - lost to Dory Funk Jr. when Funk won
          only fall achieved within hour by disq.---
          kept NWA title due to long-standing rules
**1/3/75 - beat Dick the Bruiser 2/3 falls,
          final fall via disq**
2/7/75 - beat Dory Funk Jr. 2/3 falls

12/4/70 - beat Billy [...]
          won 16-man Wrestle Royal; [...]
          Big Bill Miller in one-fall finale
1/1/71 - one-hour draw with Dory Funk, Jr.
1/15/71 - went to 20-min. draw with Pak-Son
as survivors of 6-man tag elim. bout; beat
Hans Schmidt on own - with O'Connor and Jones
against Schmidt, Pak-Son and Anderson
2/5/71 - beat Pak-Son
2/19/71 - with Bruiser beat Pak-Son-Schmidt;
          pinned Schmidt for only fall
3/5/71 - lost to Black Jack Lanza
3/19/71 - drew with Big Bill Miller

[...] Gene Kiniski 2/3 falls
11/16/73 - beat Terry Funk 2/3 falls (2nd fall
          win on disqualification)

at Kiel - Friday, February 19, 1971 (att. 8317)

Dory Funk, Jr. retained title by beating Von
Raschke. 1st fall-Funk won with spinning toehold
7:35. 2nd fall-Raschke won with the Iron claw
1:54. 3rd fall-Funk won with a Japanese wrist-
lock 5:43.
Jack Brisco and Dick the Bruiser beat Pak-Son and
Hans Schmidt when Brisco beat Schmidt with a
front rolling cradle 11:37
Pat O'Connor beat Hans Mortier with the sleeper
hold 4:59
Big Bill Miller beat Eddie Graham with a back
breaker 9:36

[...] (3)
          250   Reno, Nevada
3/3/72 - no decision with Bill Watts
3/17/72 - with O'Connor in 30 minute draw vers[...]
          Watts and Lanza
4/21/72 - with O'Connor in win over Lanza and
[...]on; won 3rd fall from Pak-Son
[...]2 - pinned Jack Mulligan to win handicap
[...]out from Mulligan, Lanza & Heenan
[...]72 - beat Jack Mulligan on disqualificat[...]
[...]2 - pinned Roger Kirby to win handicap
[...] for himself and Steve Bolus
[...]2 - lost 2/3 falls to Harley Race when
[...]ered knee injury in 3rd fall

- **Bruiser vs. Black Jack Lanza** at Kiel in the late 60s. Bruiser turns from bad guy to fan favorite.
- **Harley Race vs. Johnny Valentine** at Kiel on January 19, 1973.
- **Terry Funk vs. Kiniski** at Kiel on March 16, 1973. This is the only main event Muchnick ever changed. He had scheduled Funk to wrestle Valentine, but Valentine suffered a heart attack the night before the match.
- **Jack Briscoe vs. Dory Funk Jr.** at the Arena on November 15, 1974. The two met several times in this period and they always put on a good wrestling display.
- **Race vs. Dory Funk Jr.** at Kiel in the mid-70s.
- **Harley Race vs. David Von Erich** in the early 80s at Kiel and the Arena.
- **Bruiser vs. Ric Flair** at Kiel on June 12, 1982.
- **Andre the Giant vs. King Kong Brody** at Kiel in the early 80s.
- **Brody vs. Flair** at the Arena in a one-hour draw in the early 80s.

Sam Muchnick's file of index cards recording each of the wrestlers' participation in his promotions at the Kiel Auditorium or Wrestling at the Chase

ST. LOUIS WRESTLING HALL OF FAME ALUMNI

THE ST. LOUIS WRESTLING HALL OF FAME is dedicated to those who made St. Louis the capital of professional wrestling. As Larry Matysik stated at the opening of the Hall of Fame in 2007, "Had St. Louis not accepted wrestling on television as it did, the sport might never have developed as it has over the decades."

Bill Apter, 2015
Journalist

Bob Backlund, 2017
Wrestler

Penny Banner, 2007
Wrestler

Jack Brisco, 2008
Wrestler

King Kong Brody, 2007
Wrestler

Dick the Bruiser, 2007
Wrestler

Édouard Carpentier, 2017
Wrestler

Debbie Combs, 2019
Wrestler

Ted DiBiase, 2014
Wrestler

"Cowboy" Bob Ellis, 2010
Wrestler

Ric Flair, 2007
Wrestler

Dory Funk Jr., 2008
Wrestler

Terry Funk, 2010
Wrestler

Joe Garagiola, 2008
Commentator

Mickey Garagiola, 2007
Ring Announcer

Rip Hawk, 2014
Wrestler

Bobby Heenan, 2010
Manager

John Paul Henning, 2016
Wrestler

Rocky Johnson, 2008
Wrestler

Gene Kiniski, 2007
Wrestler

Wild Bill Logsdon, 2007
Wrestler

Larry Matysik, 2007
Commentator

Big Bill Miller, 2016
Wrestler

Sam Muchnick, 2007
Promoter

Dick Murdoch, 2010
Wrestler

Pat O'Connor, 2007
Wrestler

Bob Orton Sr., 2019
Wrestler

Ken Patera, 2015
Wrestler

Harley Race, 2007
Wrestler

Buddy Rogers, 2008
Wrestler

Joe Schoenberger, 2007
Referee

Ed Smith, 2015
Wrestler/Referee

Wilbur Snyder, 2014
Wrestler

Joe Tangaro, 2015
Wrestler

Lou Thesz, 2007
Wrestler

Charles Venator, 2016
Referee

Johnny Valentine, 2007
Wrestler

Fritz Von Erich, 2007
Wrestler

Kerry Von Erich, 2016
Wrestler

Kevin Von Erich, 2016
Wrestler

David Von Erich, 2016
Wrestler

Baron Von Raschke, 2009
Wrestler

Lee Warren, 2008
Referee

Whipper Billy Watson, 2018
Wrestler

TODAY'S WRESTLERS FOLLOWING THE *WRESTLING AT THE CHASE* TRADITION!

CURTIS WYLDE AND WYLDEFYRE

FLASH FLANAGAN

NIGHT TRAIN GARY JACKSON

GUERILLA WARFARE (BIG TEXAN AND WACO)

FRANKIE D

AMBASSADOR SEAN VINCENT

SUPERSTAR STEVE FENDER

THE PROFESSIONALS (MAULER MCDARBY AND SEAN SANTEL)

ATTILA KAHN WITH TRAVIS COOK

BILLY MCNEIL

CHRISTOPHER HARGAS

KOWALSKI

ACKNOWLEDGMENTS

AS NOTED, THIS IS A BOOK of memories. It comprises memories and events that took place in a wrestling ring and inside the homes of countless fans across the Midwest. Many people came forth to share their stories. However, the person who had the greatest impact on this book is Herb Simmons. He is the torchbearer of old-time wrestling, having taken the third handoff in life's race—from Sam Muchnick to Larry Matysik to Herb. It is through Herb that the films that document professional wrestling in St. Louis still exist, and he generously opened up those archives and shared them along with his own personal experiences. Without him, this work would not have been possible.

As noted throughout this book, *Wrestling at the Chase*'s foundation was supported by three legs: the location, the delivery, and the product. Both Ted, Bob, and Sam Koplar provided insight into their family's role in providing the opulent location to host the event, as well as the dynamic means to transmit it to everyone's home. And then there was Sam Muchnick, the mentor to Larry and Herb who provided the promotions that made it all happen. His children Dick and Kathy provided insights into a man who was almost bigger than life—not because of what he accomplished but how he accomplished it. Bob Garagiola was there to relive the stories of his father, Mickey, the ambassador of both *Wrestling at the Chase* and the Hill. There were others like Larry Matysik's wife, Pat, and the many fans and wrestlers who responded to our questionnaire. And finally there were special friends who helped throughout the process by providing support while adding pieces to the story as well as important memorabilia. These include Jim Anderson, Bob Costas, Jim Fetsch, Joe Holleman, Mark Kern, Cody Knipping, Randy Liebler, Vicki Martin, Irene and Tom Mueller, Rich Noffke, Nick Rednour, Kara Vaninger, and Brian Walsh. Like so many others, they have vivid memories of special Saturday nights and Sunday mornings, and with their help we will all keep the legacy of *Wrestling at the Chase* alive for years to come.

ENDNOTES

1. Lobbia, J.A., "Chased into History," *Chicago Tribune*, September 24, 1989, Section 5, p. 7.
2. Lobbia, J.A., "Chased into History," *Chicago Tribune*, September 24, 1989, Section 5, p. 7.
3. O'Connor, Candace, *Meet Me in the Lobby: The Story of Harold Koplar & the Chase Park Plaza*. Virginia Publishing Co., 2005, p. 17.
4. Schildroth, Keith, "From 1930 to 1970 Kiel Was Wrestling Capital," *St. Louis Post-Dispatch*, March 3, 1991, Section F, p. 6.
5. Kusch, Kyle, The Basement Geographer, licensed under the Creative Commons Attribution 2.0 Generic license, 2011.
6. Thesz, Lou, with Kit Bauman, *Hooker: An Authentic Wrestler's Adventures inside the Bizarre World of Professional Wrestling*, Wrestling Channel Press: 2001, p. 45.
7. Matysik, Larry, *Wrestling at the Chase, The Inside Story of Sam Muchnick and the Legends of Professional Wrestling*. ECW Press, 2005, p. 15.
8. Matysik, Larry, *Wrestling at the Chase, The Inside Story of Sam Muchnick and the Legends of Professional Wrestling*. ECW Press, 2005, p. 15.
9. Matysik, Larry, W*restling at the Chase, The Inside Story of Sam Muchnick and the Legends of Professional Wrestling*. ECW Press, 2005, p. 16.
10. Quinn, Kay, "The Man Who Brought Television to St. Louis," https://www.ksdk.com/article/news/history/happy-73rd-birthday-ksdk-history-television-st-louis/63-455d568e-e2c2-4657-b195-800798271ba7, 2020.
11. Quinn, Kay, "The Man Who Brought Television to St. Louis," https://www.ksdk.com/article/news/history/happy-73rd-birthday-ksdk-history-television-st-louis/63-455d568e-e2c2-4657-b195-800798271ba7, 2020.
12. "TV Announcer Hurt in Auto Plunge," *St. Louis Globe-Democrat*, August 14, 1963, Section A, p. 8.
13. "Announcer's Death Laid to Barbiturates, Alcohol," S*t. Louis Post-Dispatch*, December 16, 1964, p. 4.
14. Matysik, Larry, *Wrestling at the Chase, The Inside Story of Sam Muchnick and the Legends of Professional Wrestling*. ECW Press, 2005, p. 225.
15. Futterman, Ellen, "America Grapples with Wrestling," *St. Louis Post-Dispatch*, January 9, 2000, Section A, p. 1.
16. Johnson, Mike, "Exclusive: Billy Corgan Finalizes Deal to Purchase . . .," Pro *Wrestling Insider*, May 1, 2017.
17. Matysik, Larry, *Wrestling at the Chase, The Inside Story of Sam Muchnick and the Legends of Professional Wrestling*. ECW Press, 2005, p. 158.
18. Matysik, Larry, *Wrestling at the Chase, The Inside Story of Sam Muchnick and the Legends of Professional Wrestling*. ECW Press, 2005, p. 157.
19. Matysik, Larry, *Wrestling at the Chase, The Inside Story of Sam Muchnick and the Legends of Professional Wrestling*. ECW Press, 2005, p. 157.
20. Thesz, Lou, with Kit Bauman, *Hooker: An Authentic Wrestler's Adventures inside the Bizarre World of Professional Wrestling*, Wrestling Channel Press: 2001, pp. 95–96.
21. Matysik, Larry, *Wrestling at the Chase, The Inside Story of Sam Muchnick and the Legends of Professional Wrestling*. ECW Press, 2005, p. 73.
22. Schildroth, Keith, "Muchnick's Most Memorable Wrestling Cards," *St. Louis Post-Dispatch*, January 4, 1999, Section C, p. 4.

The faces of *Wrestling at the Chase*

INDEX